I Need a Lifeguard Everywhere but the Pool

I Need a Lifeguard Everywhere but the Pool

Lisa Scottoline

&

Francesca Serritella

ST. MARTIN'S PRESS 🐾 NEW YORK

www.stmartins.com

All photographs courtesy of the authors except where indicated.

The Library of Congress Cataloging-in-Publication Data is available upon request.

ISBN 978-1-250-05996-3 (hardcover)
ISBN 978-1-4668-6526-6 (e-book)

Our books may be purchased in bulk for promotional, educational, or business use. Please contact your local bookseller or the Macmillan Corporate and Premium Sales Department at 1-800-221-7945, extension 5442, or by e-mail at MacmillanSpecialMarkets@macmillan.com.

First Edition: July 2017

10 9 8 7 6 5 4 3 2 1

To Laura Leonard, with love and gratitude

Contents

I Need a Lifeguard Everywhere but the Pool

Introduction

Lisa

Welcome to our collection of funny stories about our everyday lives, which will sound like your everyday lives, except less well behaved.

We're a mother-daughter team who also happens to be best friends—as well as occasional enemies.

What mother has not had a daughter slam a door in her face?

What daughter has not had a mother roll her eyes behind her back?

We're talking about family in these stories, and we keep it real.

Real funny.

We each write about our lives from our differing perspectives. Francesca is a thirtysomething in an apartment in New York City, and I live on a farm in Pennsylvania. As far as my age goes, let's just say I can't remember the last time I had estrogen.

I prefer it on the rocks.

Francesca came up with the title of this book, and as soon as she said it, we both knew it was perfect.

I need a lifeguard everywhere *but* the pool.

Haven't we all felt that way, sometimes?

Especially me, because I can't even swim.

Yet I have a pool.

Every summer, I get out to my pool for an hour a day and try not to drown.

I flail, I doggie-paddle, I put my face under the water, and somehow, I don't die.

I wish there were a lifeguard, but there isn't.

Do you smell a metaphor?

Isn't that what life is like, at times?

I'm divorced twice, from Thing One and Thing Two, and Francesca isn't dating anyone right now. In fact, as you will read in her stories herein, she's on what she calls a "guyatus"—a hiatus from guys.

So here we are, mother and daughter, happily single yet unhappily celibate, going through life on our own.

We're not the only ones. There are a lot of women in our position, whether divorced, widowed, or just never got married or divorced in the first place.

And we still count.

Even if you're lucky enough to be in full-blown love, marriage, or living with someone in unwedded bliss, there are going to be times in your life when you are simply on your own.

When no matter how much someone loves you, they can't undergo chemo for you, or get you out of debt, or help you make a decision that is personal to you.

I grew up in an era when women expected to be saved by a Prince Charming.

Which is just another kind of lifeguard.

But with a castle.

And I don't think that those expectations have completely left this culture. I think the myth of Prince Charming, a lifeguard, or Mr. Right to make everything right, is as pervasive as ever.

And that notion can make you unhappy if you don't have one, or if you think other women have one and you don't.

But here's what I want you to know:

As I lived a little, I began to understand that there was no Prince Charming—and that wasn't bad news.

On the contrary, it's excellent news to be on your own.

Who better to trust with your life than you?

Who knows you better than you know yourself?

Who's more reliable than a woman?

The busier we are, the more we get done.

We haven't met the Things To Do List we can't defeat.

We were born to check boxes.

You're a grown-ass woman, and you make excellent decisions.

If you want the job done right, do it yourself.

Right?

So there is no lifeguard in life.

Though sometimes we wish for one, mightily. By the way, it's okay to secretly whine about the fact you don't have one, just so long as you understand that you don't really need one.

You will get to the other side of the pool even if you can't swim.

Sometimes life is treading water and not going anywhere.

You won't sink, girl.

Think of your breasts as a flotation device.

And your hips and your butt, in my case.

Bad times pass, and before you know it, it's summertime.

The sun is out, you go on vacation, and your mood lightens. You're not only staying afloat, you're making your way across the pool.

Or even the ocean.

Look back.

It's *behind* you.

Being on your own is being free.

So have a great summer.

Read this book and LOL on the beach.

The real truth is this:

You're your own lifeguard.

Ain't nobody better.

Perking Up

Lisa

Mommy has a new wish.

Besides Bradley Cooper.

We're talking coffee.

And I'm on a quest.

I know, some people climb Everest.

Others cure cancer.

But all I want is a delicious cup of coffee that I can make myself, at home.

Is that so much to ask?

Evidently.

Right out front, I have to confess that I love Dunkin' Donuts coffee.

Sometimes I'll have Starbucks and other times Wawa, but my coffee soul mate is Dunkin'.

We've been together longer than either of my marriages combined.

Daughter Francesca likes to tell the story of the time we were watching television and a Dunkin' Donuts commercial came on, and I whispered, "I love you, Dunkin' Donuts."

Okay, that's embarrassing enough.

But then Francesca tweeted that to Dunkin' Donuts, and Dunkin' Donuts tweeted back:

"We love you too, Lisa!"

OMG!!!!!

Anyway, you get the idea.

So I stop by Dunkin' Donuts whenever I can and I also pick up a lottery ticket. When I lose the lottery, at least I've had a great cup of coffee, which makes me almost as happy.

You're supposed to be able to make Dunkin' Donuts at home, and I have a Keurig coffeemaker, so I bought the Dunkin' Donuts K-Cups and did the whole Keurig thing, but it wasn't the same as the real thing.

And unfortunately, I developed almost a superstitious belief that a cup of great coffee is essential to my writing process. I'm not the first writer to believe that a beverage is essential to great fiction. Ernest Hemingway had booze, but I have caffeine. And when my good-luck charm is on shaky ground, I fear my books will start to suck, and Mrs. Bradley Cooper can't have that.

So I decided that I would give up on making Dunkin' Donuts at home and try different types of coffee. I understand this is called being flexible, but it's not something that comes easily to me.

Nor should it.

One of the great things about being single is that you never have to compromise anything, and I wasn't looking forward to compromising my one and only vice.

Nevertheless, I decided I should go back to basics, namely percolated coffee. I admit this was probably nostalgia-driven, because I remember the days when Mother Mary perked coffee on the stovetop, brewing Maxwell House from a can, but I couldn't find a stovetop percolator and had to settle for a plug-in, and I thought I could beat Maxwell House, so I got myself to the grocery store, where I stood before a dizzying array of types of coffee, coming from everywhere around the globe, including Africa, Arabia, and the Pacific.

This was coffee with frequent-flyer mileage.

Likewise there were different kinds of roasts—light, dark, French, Italian, and Extra Dark French, which sounded vaguely racist.

I went with medium Italian, because that's basically what I am.

Then I had to choose the "body" of the coffee, which evidently meant "the weight of the coffee on your tongue."

Everywhere you look, body issues.

Again I chose the light-to-medium bodied, ground it at the store, brought it home, perked it, and it sucked. I persevered for another week, but I couldn't do it. I decided to throw out the baby with the coffee water and went back further to my roots to buy a little Italian Bialetti espresso maker, perked on the stovetop. But that meant I had to go back to the grocery store and start all over again, since the new coffeemaker required the moka grind, which is not even a word.

I brought the coffee home, perked it, and took a sip.

It sucked, too.

Or maybe I suck at flexibility.

So now I don't know what to do.

I'm taking any and all suggestions.

And I have a novel to finish.

Tell me how to make a great cup of coffee.

The future of literature depends upon it.

Also my job.

I'll split the Powerball with you.

We're Having a Baby!

Francesca

I was hunched over my laptop, reading an article about which baby stroller is best for city dwellers, when my mom peered over my shoulder.

"Do you have something to tell me?"

We're having a baby!

Well, my friend group is.

I've been part of a stable group of six, dear girlfriends since we were in the sixth grade, and now the first of us is pregnant. We've moved through many steps of life in stride, but a baby is a new frontier.

I am beyond excited.

Last night I couldn't sleep, my brain was too busy thinking of baby names.

Don't worry, I would never be so presumptuous as to suggest any.

(But in case she's reading this: if you're curious, I have a list, and it's totally okay if you hate them, but I'm just gonna email . . .)

In addition to researching strollers, I've scoured Sephora reviews of the best stretch-mark cream and scouted the coolest maternity clothes websites. I've pre-selected my friend's birth-day, Christmas, and Groundhog Day presents.

And I haven't even gotten started on gifts for the baby.

Actually, I take that back—I did preorder a board book entitled *Feminist Baby,* because I'm staking my claim as *that* aunt early.

Thanks to my web search history, every online advertise-ment thinks I'm pregnant.

If I see one more pop-up for breast pumps . . .

Last week, the New York contingent of our girl gang got dinner with Mama for the first time since she emailed us all the happy news.

The moment she slipped off her coat and revealed the ti-niest baby bump, I girl-squealed.

And I never girl-squeal.

I found myself making sure she sat out of the way of the passing busboys, wanting to pull the chair out for her, then wanting the waiter to bring water faster, and bread, lots of bread! I wanted to order everything on the menu and watch her eat it.

Even as her friend, seeing her triggered an animal urge to nurture and protect her.

Our pride is having its first cub, and we lionesses need to circle the den.

When the waiter brought the wine list, we waved him off. It went without saying that we were abstaining in solidarity.

We made about two minutes of small chat before I caved and said, "SO, what is it like?" and we unleashed a torrent of questions.

Pregnancy is simultaneously the most universal female experience and the most unfathomable one. You can't possibly imagine what it's really like until you experience it.

Or, second best, until you see it up close.

And until this moment, I've only gotten as close as a sonogram photo on Facebook.

I'm an only child, and in my small extended family, I have only one cousin—and he's older. On both sides, the Scottolines and Serritellas are bad at reproduction.

No one can stay married long enough.

I babysat the neighbor's kids as a teenager, but actual infants were above my pay grade.

I've cooed over babies but never held one.

Pip doesn't count.

When I've had an acquaintance or distant relative announce a pregnancy, I congratulate them, but I don't feel comfortable asking any questions. I never know what is and isn't polite to ask, it seems too personal.

But nothing is too personal between friends of twenty years. So I had a million questions at this dinner.

How do you feel? Are you nauseous? Are you starving?

Are your boobs awesome now? Oh no, they *hurt*?!?

When does it kick?

Does this mean we can order dessert?

She laughed and patiently answered our questions and filled us in on all the things that she did and didn't expect. She told us the best news ever:

It's a girl!

I tried not to immediately burst into tears. I nearly succeeded.

It was at once surreal and fitting that I was again leaning

over a table with these girlfriends to learn about this most momentous experience of womanhood, just like we had when we were sitting around the lunch table in middle school, comparing notes on the most trivial firsts of womanhood.

These are the girls with whom I puzzled out puberty. Together, we figured out which razors wouldn't nick your knees, even with a shaky hand, which maxi pads felt least like diapers, which tampons were the least scary. They reassured me that I was not the only girl on earth to have slightly unequal-sized breasts.

Whoever did anything first had to report back to the troops. We compared notes on what to do with your tongue when you kiss. When the first of us saw a guy naked, lunch break became a *Grey's Anatomy* lesson, complete with crude diagrams drawn on the back of a napkin.

And it wasn't just boy stuff, we conferred on SAT prep, college essays; anything big and daunting was tackled as a team.

After college, we no longer hit life milestones in lockstep with one another. That can be a source of jealousy or angst in some friendships, but only if you reduce major life events like marriage or a child to merit badges of womanhood.

I have truly never felt competitive with these friends, but I think that's because we always helped each other.

Childbearing is more complicated than shaving your legs. It will probably take all six of us to get a comprehensive sense of this remarkable, insane, beautiful female experience.

Friendship is like a longitudinal study of how to be human. We're here to be each other's test subjects, and to use our findings to tip the scales toward happiness.

Not that Mama is our unlucky guinea pig—it evens out. Yes, she's running the diaper gauntlet first. But she has all of us unencumbered single ladies around to support her. Her baby girl will be the object of adoration of five happy aunties and last-minute babysitters.

Those of us who have children later won't need as much help, since we'll have cribbed notes for years. Plus, we'll get the mother lode of hand-me-down baby clothes.

And if any of us is unsure that having kids is right for her, she'll have five of us living, breathing, spit-up-covered pros-and-cons lists to help her decide.

For the last twenty years, these girls, now women, have been my brain trust. Thanks to them, for the last two decades I haven't had to figure anything out alone.

And Baby Girl, you will always have a high chair at our table.

Spot On

Lisa

It turns out that my past is spotty.

And yours may be, too.

I learned this when I turned sixty.

(I'm still getting used to saying that, much less seeing it in print.)

All of us women have to cope with the signs of aging, and some of us do so better than others.

I mostly ignore it.

I'm not a model, so I don't earn a living by the way I look, and I've come to like my face, even with its laugh lines, since I like to laugh.

I know that sometimes my cheeks look drawn and hollow, which is the kind of thing that tempts some women to opt for injections of filler.

I don't judge, but that isn't my style.

As soon as I hear "injections," I'm gone.

And the only filler my face needs is carbohydrates.

The same is true of face-lifts or cosmetic surgery. I don't blame anybody who does it, but my fear kicks in at "surgery."

Though I have to admit that I've been tempted recently,

a fact I discovered by accident. After summer was over, I noticed an oddly dark spot on my cheek, and since I wasn't always careful about using sunscreen, I worried it was cancer. The very notion sent me scurrying to the Internet, where I looked at various horrifying slides and learned the acronym ABCDE, which stands for asymmetry, border, color, diameter, and evolving.

Now you learned something, and so did I.

The last time I had memorized an acronym with as much interest was when I was getting engaged, and I learned about the four C's for engagement rings.

Cut, clarity, color, carat.

Much more fun.

Worried, I called around and found a dermatologist, a woman reputed to be a great doctor, though on the brusque side.

In other words, a woman of few words.

I hadn't even known such a creature existed.

Obviously, she's the direct opposite of me, but I wasn't looking for love, just to stay alive.

Anyway, the dermatologist suggested that I come in for a mole check.

I agreed, though she'd said it so fast, I thought she'd said "mold check."

Which was probably more accurate.

I'm not getting old, I'm getting mold.

Or maybe I'm molting.

Either way, I went to the dermatologist, who examined the suspicious mole and determined it was benign.

Yay!

I promised myself never to skip the sunscreen, ever again.

But then the dermatologist frowned behind the contraption that magnified her eyes to two brown marbles. She pointed to my temples and said, "You have quite a lot of keratoses."

Again I didn't understand because she was looking at my forehead, not my toesies. "What did you say?"

"These brownish spots on your temples. You have so many."

Thanks, I thought, but didn't say. "They're from the sun, aren't they?"

"No, that's a common misconception. They're hereditary."

I remembered then that my father used to have them, which might have been the reason I never minded them. Because they reminded me of him.

The dermatologist said, "They're not related to age, but they age you, and I can remove them."

"Really?"

"Hold on." The dermatologist left the office, then returned with a styrofoam cup of what looked like coffee, because a curlicue of steam wafted from inside the cup. Before I could understand what was going on, she swiped a Q-tip inside the cup and pressed it to my temple.

"Ow," I blurted out. "What is that?"

"Liquid nitrogen. It burns, right?"

"Right." I bit my lip as she swiped the Q-tip back in the styrofoam cup and pressed it on a few other places on my temples.

I wanted my mommy, but didn't say so.

Because that would have been immature.

The dermatologist finished up, saying, "That's all for now. Call my office in a week or so and make an appointment to remove the others."

I thanked her and left the office, my forehead a field of red dots, like a constellation that spelled out:

WE AGE YOU

A week later, the red dots had turned brown and fallen off, and in their place was fresh pink skin.

I could see that I looked better, maybe even younger.

But I have to say, I missed looking like my father.

And I think I'll leave the other ones alone.

Recipe Ambition

Lisa

Everybody knows that the holidays are crazy busy.

But what we don't know is why we make them busier.

Or rather, why I do.

I begin by saying that as of this writing, there are less than two weeks left before Christmas and I have not begun to shop. I've bought some gifts online but I still want to go into an actual store, not only because it's fun, but because I want actual stores to remain open.

This is one thing I've learned in my dotage.

If you want something to exist, you have to support it with actual money. So as much as I love to shop online, I make sure I spend my money in the bricks and mortar.

Vote with your boots.

And your bucks.

So you would naturally think that this is a story about me going shopping for gifts, but it isn't. Because at about the same time, I decided to try a really unusual holiday meal for Christmas.

The holidays are the time for Recipe Ambition.

Please tell me that I'm not the only one who decides that

the busiest time of the year is the perfect time to make the fanciest recipe ever, for the first time.

It's worth noting that I first had this idea for Thanksgiving, but I got too tired.

But now that Christmas is coming up, I wanted to give my Recipe Ambition a trial run. The last thing you want to do is cook a new dish at Christmas and have it fall through, so that you end up serving cereal with a side of beer.

And since Francesca and I are vegetarians, we're always looking for something to substitute for turkey, and our days of Tofurkey are over. No disrespect, but Tofurkey reminds you that you want real turkey and we're making a clean break.

In other words, we're going cold turkey on Tofurkey.

I had been reading my recipe books and feeling my Italian heritage, which is the kind of thing that happens at the holidays, when I get nostalgic for hard-core ethnic food that no one in my family ever made, because we got too tired.

Which brings me to fava beans.

You may not have heard of them, except that if you watched Hannibal Lecter, you know he likes fava beans with liver.

But like I say, we're vegetarians.

I had fava beans when Francesca and I went to Italy, and they were hearty and delicious, so when I was in the grocery store before Thanksgiving, I decided they would be my Recipe Ambition. The beans were large, hard, and an ugly green-brown, kept loose in a plastic container that had an opening on the bottom, which I had never used before. I got a plastic bag, put it under the opening, and released the lever, which was when a zillion beans poured into my bag, clattering like an organic jackpot.

It was way too many but I couldn't figure out how to pour them back.

People were looking at me, and I felt stupid, so I got a twist tie, labeled the beans, and bought them. I had a recipe on how to make them, and they're easy to make, but none of the recipes kick in until you get the bean out of the skin.

One recipe actually said, "It's mainly because shelling fava beans can be such tedious work that making this soup becomes an act of love."

Now you tell me?

Tedious doesn't even begin to explain the process of shelling fava beans.

Tedious is foreplay.

Especially when you bought a zillion of them.

Only 52,095 more to go!

And you can't begin to shell them until after you soak them overnight, and I even found a recipe that you have to soak them for six days.

This was more Italian than I can deal with.

So I soaked them for five hours, which was all the hours I had left in the day, and that barely loosened up the skin, so I had to start scraping with my fingernails, a paring knife, and at one point, a corkscrew.

I was trying to figure out the easiest way to do it.

Turns out the easiest way is not to bother.

But I was not about to be beaten by a bean.

So I turned on the football game and started shelling. I had shelled enough to make whatever I was going to make after about two hours, forty-five beans, and two bloody cuts.

I took the unshelled beans, put them in a Ziploc bag, and froze them, which means I will forget about them until next year.

And I went to the mall.

Our Ladies of Perpetual Motion

Lisa

I'm delighted to hear that Mother Teresa is going to be made a saint.

But I'm also surprised.

That she wasn't already.

I mean, what does it take?

Before I begin, please understand that I'm not criticizing the Catholic Church. This is a humor column, and I'm Catholic myself. Of course it goes without saying that Mother Teresa is incredibly inspiring, but looked at another way, there's nobody like Mother Teresa to make you feel inadequate, especially in the holiday season.

At this time of year, if you're like me, you're trying to do your actual job while you juggle shopping, wrapping, planning a big meal, and hoping to remember where you put the tree stand.

Nobody remembers where they put the tree stand.

The tree stand is the cell phone of the holiday season.

The only problem is, you can't call it.

Worse yet is trying to find the tree skirt.

Yes, I own a tree skirt.

I don't wear skirts anymore, but my tree does. When it starts to wear panty hose, we're all in trouble.

But anyway, my point is that in the holiday season, I'm working at maximum capacity and still falling far short. For example, I'm writing this just a few days before Christmas, but I haven't figured out what I'm going to make for dinner, so I haven't gone food shopping, and I haven't gotten a tree yet, so I'm guaranteed to end up with one that's crappy and expensive, which reminds me of my second marriage.

But to get back to Mother Teresa, I can barely deal with the holiday season, and after all the gifts have been opened, the big meal eaten, and the dishes washed, I can tell you that I will feel like a saint.

Saint Lisa, Our Lady of Perpetual Motion.

I'm sure I'm not alone in this. If you are responsible for staging a holiday in your household, you probably feel like a saint, and in my view, you are one.

No matter what your religion.

Every woman can be a martyr.

It's a God-given right, no matter which God you believe in.

So when I heard that Mother Teresa was finally about to attain sainthood, I started to look into what she had done to qualify. First, she was born in Macedonia, which is not near any mall that I know of.

So right there, if you ask me, she's on the fast track to sainthood.

She became a nun at eighteen and traveled to India, where

she was so moved by the poverty that she experienced what she termed "a call within the call." She became "a free nun covered with the poverty of the cross," so she gave up her nun's habit and put on a white sari.

Any woman who wears white deserves sainthood.

In fact, Mother Teresa may be the only woman whoever looked thin in white.

Me, I never wear white.

In white, I look like a glacier.

Mother Teresa lived among the poor, caring for them, even begging for them.

You know me, and the only begging I'm doing is for Bradley Cooper.

Mother Teresa started the Missionaries of Charity, dedicated to caring for "the hungry, the naked, the homeless, the crippled, the blind, the lepers, all those people who feel unwanted, unloved, uncared for throughout society, people that have become a burden to the society and are shunned by everyone."

Wow.

The only people I'm caring for this holiday season are the hungry.

And by that I mean Daughter Francesca and bestie Franca, who'll be at my house for the holiday meal. And even at that, Francesca will help with the cooking and Franca will bring the dessert, because really, enough already.

As for lepers, I admit I'm avoiding them.

I need all my fingers.

For my rings.

Mother Teresa helped children trapped in war in Beirut,

radiation victims at Chernobyl, and earthquake victims in Armenia.

Okay, but has she ever stood in line at Nordstrom's, trying to get a box for a sale sweater?

Or on line at Starbucks, waiting for overpriced caffeine?

I have.

Where's my medal?

Mother Teresa continued her good works despite two heart attacks, pneumonia, and malaria.

Sadly, I think I'm getting a cold.

For her decades of charitable work, Mother Teresa was awarded the Nobel Peace Prize in 1979.

But that still wasn't enough for sainthood.

To qualify for sainthood, you have to perform not only one, but two miracles.

And toughest yet, you have to do them after you're dead.

Look, I understand that we're talking about sainthood here, but that's not a standard that many women meet, especially not this woman.

I have only one miracle up my sleeve, and I will perform it on Christmas Day, when I make actual cranberry sauce from scratch, and don't serve the canned kind with those ridges on the sides.

So while I am inspired by Mother Teresa, I'm not her.

And I'm wishing happy holidays to everyone, all of the ordinary people who perform ordinary miracles, every day.

You're all saints to me.

New Year's Meh

Francesca

I have about a month before I turn thirty, so I'm on the lookout for unwelcome signs of wisdom and maturity. What I noticed this week:

I've stopped caring about New Year's Eve.

Not in a bah-humbug way, but it just doesn't have the hold on me that it used to.

New Year's Eve is like the rare ex-boyfriend with whom I've achieved genuine friendship—we have an okay time in each other's company, but I don't bother trying to look devastatingly beautiful around him anymore.

It's a big step for me. I used to put enormous effort into having a good time on New Year's Eve. I had to have the Best Night Ever™, ideally with plenty of witnesses and photo documentation.

And I was unwilling to admit defeat. My senior year of high school, my girlfriends and I went out to a nice prix fixe dinner. I wasn't feeling too good after eating the lobster salad, but my then-boyfriend was throwing a party, and I was wearing my new, sequin shrug—remember when shrugs were a thing?—I was going to be seen. With increasing queasiness, I sweated it out until eleven, when my best friend had to take me home.

We stopped twice for me to puke along the side of the road.

By the time the ball dropped, I was Linda Blair in *The Exorcist*.

It got so bad, my mom took me to the ER.

Imagine you're a seventeen-year-old girl sick to the point of passing out on New Year's Eve, and then imagine trying to convince jaded ER docs that you *aren't* drunk.

After initial skepticism and several blood tests, I was diagnosed with toxicity poisoning from a bad lobster. I almost wished it had been champagne.

But I achieved my wish of staying up all night—on IV fluids.

My sophomore year of college, my best friend took me as her plus-one to a fancy cocktail party her friends were throwing in New York City. We took the train in, got a hotel room (that our moms probably paid for), primped like it was prom, and headed out on one of the coldest New Year's Eves in memory.

At twenty years old, we felt incredibly grown-up—we were in formal dresses with older boys in the big city, and I was utterly certain that this was the first night of our glamorous adult lives.

Plus, I'd recently broken up with my high-school sweetheart and the only boy I'd ever kissed, so I was determined to find new love on the most romantic night of the year.

Finding true love took longer than I expected.

Fast-forward to 3:30 A.M. the first morning of the New Year, the two of us shivering on the sidewalk, our legs frozen numb, but our feet on fire after hours in high heels. We were waiting much too politely as cab after cab went to different people.

So I improvised.

Unable to withstand the pain of my shoes a minute longer, I dug plastic bags out of the trash and tied them to my feet.

Hobbling in my bag slippers, we managed to hail an off-duty party bus and beg the driver to take us back to our hotel.

He took pity on us—it was the shoes.

But if that isn't a dedication to having fun on NYE, I don't know what is.

Over time, my desperate need to do the coolest and hippest thing has subsided. The invisible audience judging my social life has dispersed. And the resulting quiet makes it easier to focus on what I cherish every year.

Like last year, I spent the holiday with my best friend— the same girl who held my hair back and also helped me find clean takeout bags for my feet—only instead we celebrated by sitting on the couch in my mother's house, giggling at our old high-school yearbooks.

It was one of my favorite New Year's Eves.

This year, the most tantalizing invite I received was from a close friend throwing a "New Year's Eve Stay-In" at his apartment.

A small group of friends in a room quiet enough to hear them talk? Sounds perfect.

I no longer need champagne and sequins to have a great night. The calmer celebrations may not yield the crazy stories or the false envy on Instagram, but my ego will survive. And my heart will be happy.

Happy New Year!

Lift and Separate

Lisa

Once again, you've come to the right place.

If you read this, you're going to LOL.

But this time, I can't take the credit.

Sometimes the world hands you an ace. All you have to do is set it down on the table and play.

I'm talking, of course, about the SmartBra.

Have you heard about this? If not, I'm here to tell you that at the recent consumer electronics show, a Canadian tech company introduced a smart bra, which is a bra that is smarter than you are.

Or at least smarter than your breasts.

Microsoft is reportedly developing a smart bra, too, and I'm sure the other tech companies will follow suit.

Or maybe bra.

If it creeps you out that the male-dominated tech industry is thinking about what's under your shirt, raise your hand.

Just don't raise it very fast.

They're watching you jiggle.

Bottom line, the smartbras contain sensors that are supposed to record your "biometric data" and send it to an app on your mobile device.

It's a fitbit for your breasts.

Or a fittit.

Sorry, I know that's rude, but I couldn't resist.

Like I said, the world handed me an ace.

Anyway, to stay on point, the biometric data it monitors is your heart rate and respiration rate, but Microsoft has taken that a step further. According to CNN, their smartbra is embedded with "psychological sensors that seek to monitor a woman's heart activity to track her emotional moods and combat overeating." In fact, their "sensors can signal the wearer's smartphone, which then flash [sic] a warning message to help her step away from the fridge and make better diet decisions."

Isn't that a great idea?

It's a bra that tells on you when you're hitting the chocolate cake.

Forgive me if I'm not rushing out to buy one.

I already know when I'm being bad, and I don't need to be nagged by my underwear.

By the way, the smart bra sells for $150.

If that price gives you a heart attack, the bra will know it.

Maybe the bra can call 911.

Maybe the bra can even drive you to the hospital.

Don't slack, bra.

That's for breasts.

The Canadian company says that wearable tech is the latest thing, and that it developed its smart bra because it had "a plethora of requests from eager women who wanted in on the action, too."

Do you believe that?

I don't.

On the contrary, I know a plethora of eager women who wish they didn't have to wear a bra at all.

I also know a plethora of eager women who take their bra off the moment they hit the house.

Plus I know a plethora of eager women who skip the bra if they're wearing a sweatshirt, sweater, or down vest.

Finally, I know a plethora of eager women who would never use the word plethora in a sentence.

Okay, maybe I'm talking about myself.

Frankly, I don't want "in on the action" if the action means a bra that will tell the tristate area I'm pigging out.

However, I want "in on the action" if the action means Bradley Cooper.

And nobody needs a smart bra to monitor what would happen to my heart if Bradley Cooper were around.

By the way, researchers are not currently developing a pair of smart tighty-whities for men.

That's too bad because I have a name for it.

SmartBalls.

But maybe men don't need underwear with a sensor that detects their emotional changes.

They already have such a sensor.

In fact, they were born with it.

Too bad it doesn't make any noise.

Like, woohooo!

The Off Switch

Lisa

Do you remember a commercial that used to say, "Reach out and touch someone?"

If you do, you may also recall that the product they were advertising was a telephone.

Because back in the day, people needed to be encouraged to use the phone.

Let's pause for a moment of silence.

Not necessarily to mourn, but to consider how times have changed.

Because these days, you have to encourage people *not* to use the telephone. In fact, you have to beg them not to use the phone. You have to put up signs in hallways so that they won't use the phone, and you have to designate special railroad cars so they won't use the phone, and you have to pass laws so they won't use the phone while they're driving, because everybody uses the phone all the time, twenty-four/seven, nonstop.

In other words, we're reaching out.

But we're not touching anybody.

We're too busy on the phone.

We have priorities.

We're also watching TV all the time.

Do you remember when you used to have to wait a week for your favorite show to come on? The commercials called it "appointment television" and they encouraged you to "make an appointment" with your television to see your show.

Between you and me, it wasn't that hard an appointment to get.

Try and see my gynecologist.

Next year.

But to stay on point, somewhere along the line, the appointment book got thrown out the window. And we started watching TV all the time, one show after the other, all the time, twenty-four/seven, nonstop.

I do it, too.

Last night, I was watching a new television show, and as soon as it finished, a commercial came on saying that I could get the second episode right away.

But it was already midnight, and I should have been asleep by eleven.

I pressed the ON button and started watching.

I watched the whole entire second episode, half-asleep and half-awake, so that not only am I tired today, I didn't even see the stupid show.

I cannot be trusted with a TV in my room.

I've done the same thing when I watch shows on Netflix, where you don't even have to press the ON button to watch the next episode, thus eliminating that single volitional act, that tiny moment when you have a choice about watching another episode or returning to your life.

Nah.

Plus I have been known to combine these nonstop activities, and undoubtedly so have many of you, so that you can be watching your 303rd episode of The Whatever Show, while you're texting nonstop on the phone or cruising Facebook, Instagram, or Twitter nonstop.

When was the last time you were on the phone with somebody and you suspected they were scrolling through their phone during the conversation?

Or:

When was the last time you were barely listening to somebody while you were on the phone with them, because you were scrolling through your phone during the conversation?

Okay, guilty.

On both counts.

Anyway, it's very clear what the problem is here.

It's not our fault.

It's never our fault.

You could've guessed I would say that, if you have read me before.

I never blame me, or you.

This is a place where you can come and I will reliably tell you how to solve problems in your life without changing anything you do.

Leave the diets and exercise to everyone else.

This is the true judgment-free zone, and all that we need is an OFF switch.

That's the solution, right there.

If the television manufacturers would start making televisions with a big red OFF switch right in front, we would have a fighting chance.

It's their fault.

In fact, the other day, I couldn't find my remote, so I went to the television to turn it off and I couldn't even find the OFF switch. I spent fifteen minutes looking for the OFF switch on the front of the TV, then ran my fingers along its sides, feeling up my TV.

The TV enjoyed every minute.

This is what I'm telling you, it's TV manufacturers conspiring with TVs to get felt up.

With the phones, it's easy to turn off the phone, but that's part of the conspiracy.

Here's how it works:

The phone turns *itself* off, in that the calls "drop" all the time.

And what happens every time a phone call drops?

We become frenzied and call back instantly.

You could've been ending a phone conversation with somebody, but if the call gets dropped, you're going to call back instantly and spend even more time on the phone.

See, another conspiracy!

More shenanigans with the OFF switch.

Sometimes they don't give us one, and sometimes they work in mysterious ways.

It's just not our fault.

Becoming Thirty

Francesca

I'm writing this on my thirtieth birthday.

Thirty is a "milestone" birthday, but it's a confusing one, because it looks so different for different people. I have friends who are newly engaged and friends who are recently divorced, friends with kids heading to preschool and friends just entering grad school. We all made very different choices in the last decade.

I was talking about this to my best friend, a woman I've known since we were ten, and she made a good point: for most of our childhoods and our young adult lives, we hit every milestone in stride with our peers. We all learned to parallel-park, badly, around sixteen. We took turns holding each other's hair back at twenty-one. We threw our caps in the air the year after.

The sameness was reassuring. No one had to go out on a limb to grow up. It just happened to us, together.

But after college, the choose-your-own-adventure stage of life begins.

People talk about your twenties like they're a wash, a lost

When I blow out my candles for thirty tonight,
I won't be making wishes. I'll be making plans.

decade of struggle and irresponsible fun, a time capsule for
future nostalgia and regret and little else.

I did not find this to be true.

My twenties were a decade of decisions. After years of
tracked steps to choreographed achievements, I emerged from
college stunned by the terror and wonder of choice.

And it did start as terror. I was initially drawn to people
and pathways that would make my decisions for me; a part

of me wanted to be funneled into my future. Every choice seemed like an opportunity to make a mistake.

But then I just started making them, both choices and mistakes. You can't hide from decision-making forever. That life demands action is its saving grace.

So I decided where I wanted to live, what city, and what apartment. Then where I wanted to move when I couldn't live in that first place another month.

I decided what I wanted to do to make money, choosing which dream to make a professional reality and which to keep just for myself. Then I had to decide how to manage that money, what needs and treats to spend it on, and what new dreams to save up for.

I decided which friends were best for sharing drinks with and which were worthy of sharing secrets. I decided which friends would become family.

I decided which men to give my number and which ones to give my heart.

I can't say I decided whom to fall in love with, that part remains uncontrollable and magic.

But I did decide what to do after I fell in love, how to treat the men I loved so that they felt it in their bones, and how to treat them when the love wasn't enough to keep us together.

And with years of practice, I got comfortable with the business of making choices. I learned to value my own judgment as much if not more than someone else's. Of course it's important to be open to outside perspectives, but I don't think that's most young women's problem. We learn early how to view ourselves and our choices through other people's eyes.

In my twenties, I unlearned how to please everyone. I

made peace with disagreement. I didn't always know for sure that I was right, but I decided to trust myself anyway.

So it was far from some careless period—I took all of these decisions seriously. Even when I made them badly, it wasn't for lack of trying. And when I got it really right or really wrong, I took note, all the while improving my personal algorithm for happiness, compassion, and success. I was building my own life's parameters for the first time.

My twenties were filled with the heavy work of deciding the person I want to be.

My thirties will be for becoming her.

This is not to say the choices are over. I still have plenty of big ones, maybe the biggest, left to make. But I have a decade of trial and error behind me to help me decide. Now this new, wide-open decade doesn't feel so scary, it feels exciting. I know who I am, I know where I'm going, I'm ready.

So when I blow out my candles for thirty tonight, I won't be making wishes.

I'll be making plans.

Mother Mary and the Eyebrow

Lisa

Let me tell you something about Mother Mary, my late mother who is nevertheless with us in spirit, her feistiness in our hearts and her voice in our ears.

Probably like your mother's voice, except after two packs of More 100s a day.

The fact is, as feisty as Mother Mary was, she never yelled.

That may surprise you, but it's true.

My mother ruled our house and she never once raised her voice.

It was Teddy Roosevelt who said, speak softly and carry a big stick, and I'm betting he knew my mother.

She spoke softly and carried a wooden spoon.

Her spoon was like a scepter, only used for stirring gravy.

Instead of yelling, she had a series of Meaningful Facial Expressions that conveyed her will.

Chief among these was The Eyebrow.

Mother Mary used to lift, arch, and flex her right eyebrow

when she didn't like something I was doing, though she used it only when necessary, like a handgun.

The Eyebrow was meant to convey:

Cut that out.

Put that down.

Don't be fresh.

That's not funny.

Mind your own business.

Don't have so much to say.

Mother Mary also had a Major Glare that she could fire at me from the stove, which made it more potent than The Eyebrow, like a long-distance missile.

The Major Glare meant:

Don't talk that way to your brother.

Don't be so fresh.

Who are you kidding with that (action or comment)?

Where do you get off?

This last is impossible to translate. If you're from South Philly, you get it immediately. If you're not, please don't sweat it. If you can't figure it out, let it ride. No one is meant to know everything in the world.

To stay on point, the atomic bomb in Mother Mary's arsenal was The Frown.

You prayed The Frown did not come your way.

They say Italians talk with their hands, but they're wrong. They talk with their faces.

The Frown was Mother Mary's ultimate warning sign, and The Frown meant that she was going to Point Away, and if she Pointed Away, that meant that whatever you had done was so bad, you had to leave the room. She didn't care where you went, only that it was Out.

In fact, if Mother Mary said anything when she Pointed Away, it was, "Get out of my sight."

Spoken, not yelled.

My mother was not alone in believing that quiet can be more powerful than noise. The Godfather rarely spoke a whisper through three movies, except when he got to Johnny Fontane, who would try anybody's patience.

Really.

What a whiner.

Act like a man.

I bet your mother had an array of meaningful expressions, scary frowns, and lifted eyebrows, and they would come in handy in this election season.

Because every candidate is yelling.

Now listen, I'm no Pollyanna.

I know that people get angry and I'm generally a fan of emotion. And to be real, it makes great television. A debate where everybody is yelling at each other is totally fun to watch.

Until you realize that's how we choose a president.

In a country we love.

Nobody in the debates is listening to each other because they're too busy yelling. And they don't listen to the question, either. They just wait until the question is over and take it as their signal to start yelling. Then other candidates on the stage interrupt them and start yelling. Nobody listens to anybody else and nobody answers the question, and when it's over, the surrogates say it was a great debate.

The problem with yelling is that it's the same thing as bullying.

And it seems like every week there's a new debate, where we can watch candidates bully each other. And then we start to talk to each other about our views, and our voices get louder, and we start bullying each other.

It's not our fault, it's theirs.

But maybe we can stop it.

Because the last thing we want to do is act like politicians.

By the way, this is the week when we lost Antonin Scalia, who may have been the most conservative Supreme Court Justice ever, and his best friend was Ruth Bader Ginsberg, who may be the most liberal Supreme Court Justice ever.

They adored each other, though their views were very different.

The Happy Eyebrows!

It's not coincidental that neither of these people was the type to raise their voice. I have seen arguments before the Supreme Court, and although Justice Scalia's questions were pointed, he did not yell. I also heard Justice Ginsberg ask questions from the bench, and you could barely hear her.

Don't think this is because they're judges, because I've seen and heard judges yelling in court.

At me.

So what I'm saying is that true power lies in a soft voice and a listening ear.

It's okay to disagree with someone.

It's not okay to yell at them, bully them, or call them names.

And it's not okay to rejoice in anybody's death, nor is it okay to exploit that death for political gain.

I know that because I was raised right.

By The Eyebrow.

Moo

Lisa

Thank God.

Help is here.

I know, you've been worried.

You thought the world was going to hell in a handbasket.

You thought nobody cared about the serious problems we face, women in particular.

But you needn't have worried.

Because now there is a neck and chest cream.

Thank God, right?

I saw the commercial on TV a few minutes ago, and I was like, they are talking to *me*.

Specifically, my dry neck.

Which the ad called "crepey."

Like Death.

You would think we'd met!

And don't forget about my desiccated chest.

You know what's shriveling there.

The ad was too polite to say so, but I'm not.

Prune City, on both sides.

Okay, I'm exaggerating.

Raisin City.

In truth, Bilateral Raisins.

Apparently my body parts are withering away.

There are deserts with more moisture.

I did some research online and found an article that called neck-and-chest creams "décolleté creams."

Very classy.

Décolleté is French for boobs.

You can tell by the accents.

They have a French accent.

The article said, "We canvassed the market for neck and décolleté creams and found over forty products."

Forty!

Are there forty types of drugs to fight breast cancer?

Uh, no.

How about ovarian cancer?

Nope.

Are there forty types of birth-control pills?

No.

Are there even forty women CEOs in the entire country?

Sowwy.

Thank God there are forty types of boob cream.

News flash:

I don't care if my neck and my boobs age.

At least not enough to start slathering cream all over my neck and chest.

I mean, think about this.

We've gotten used to the idea that cosmetic companies sell women moisturizers for their face.

But evidently, the companies didn't make enough money.

So they started selling us neck creams.

But they still didn't make enough money.

So they went down to the chest.

Will they stop there?

What do you think?

Remember, before you answer, that this is a capitalist country.

Still.

So of course, they won't stop there.

Your dry belly is their profit center.

And don't make me go further south.

A gold mine!

If they don't stop there, where will they stop?

It's a slippery slope, ladies.

But evidently, it's not slippery enough.

Take it from me, they won't stop until we're greased pigs, head to toe.

Until every square inch of us is slathered with costly lubricants.

We'll have to shovel the goop on us with a trowel.

We won't ever be able to get dressed.

Because the emollients will never sink in.

Dogs will lick us all over.

And if we have to leave the house, we will simply lay our clothes on the floor and slither into them like girl snakes.

Because the alleged point of the creams is that they stop aging.

I saw an ad for a face-and-neck cream that said, "Turn Back the Hands of Time."

I don't mean to get all science-y on you, but that's not possible.

You know how I know?

Professor Cher taught me.

And if Cher can't turn back time, nobody can.

There is only one part of my body that gets dry enough for me to bother moisturizing.

And that's my feet.

And you know what I use on my dry feet?

It's called Bag Balm.

Not because I'm a bag.

Because it's used on cow udders.

It's made by the Dairy Association Company, has been sold since 1899, and it comes in a green tin. On the side of the tin, it reads, "After each milking, apply thoroughly and allow coating to remain on surface."

I'm not even kidding.

Because evidently all of us girls have problems with our décolleté.

The online ad for Bag Balm says, "It's not just for cows anymore!"

Now *that's* marketing.

And by that they mean, it's for dog paws.

It cost seven dollars.

It won't make any cosmetic company rich.

But if I were you, I'd buy some and skip the other creams.

After all, what do they think we are?

Boobs?

Barking up the Wrong Tree

Francesca

YOUR DOG IS BARKING
LONG AND *LOUD* AND *LATE*.
DO SOMETHING ABOUT IT.

That's what was written on a piece of paper taped to my front door in the morning.

Who left it? The note was unsigned. My apartment hallway was empty.

Most puzzling, Pip had not been barking. He had snoozed soundly in my bed in various positions around and on top of my head all night.

So, what on earth was she talking about?

I say "she" because this nasty note was written in incongruously loopy script. It was only missing the hearts dotting the i's.

Plus, the passive aggression in leaving an anonymous complaint taped to my door, when it just as easily could have been slipped underneath, said "mean girl."

This was the girl's bathroom approach to resolving neighborly conflict.

Clearly this was a misunderstanding. The most likely explanation was that she was hearing a different dog barking, one that would presumably continue barking, while she would continue to falsely accuse me and my dog. But since she hadn't signed the note, I had no way of reaching her to clear it up.

I believe there's a beagle down the hall, but I wasn't about to start pointing fingers at neighbor dogs.

I'm no snitch.

It was a preposterous accusation, I threw out the note and hoped the problem would sort itself out.

Then a terrifying thought: what if she told the co-op board?

Co-op boards in New York apartment buildings are like illuminati. No one is sure exactly who they are, but they control everything and rule by fiat. Pip and I both had to interview with a member of the board to get my apartment. My dog's politeness is a requirement for living here.

If he got a reputation for bad behavior, we could be out on the street!

The injustice of it was very upsetting. Pip is my baby, my angel, my pride and joy. He is the best-behaved dog I've ever had.

He is also the worst watchdog I have ever had.

He's almost purebred teddy bear, and he has few vestigial dog instincts. He never barks at noises outside, from other apartments, or even direct knocks on my door.

When the Chinese-food-delivery guy buzzes, he barely lifts his head off the couch and looks at me, like, "You gonna get that?"

The anti-watchdog

In fact, when my old apartment was burglarized, he was completely silent as the burglars broke my window, gathered all my Apple electronics, and left out my front door carrying my items in my *Lisa Scottoline promotional tote bag*!

If nothing else, he should have barked at the irony.

But that night, my next-door neighbors didn't hear a peep.

This was the witness-stand testimony I rehearsed in my mind.

Although I was confident in my dog's innocence, the note made me paranoid. I *felt* guilty.

Over the next few days, if he yipped once during playtime, I'd rush to shush him. I feared every neighbor I passed going in and out of the building was potentially the one who secretly hated us.

Then a few weeks later, just when we started to get comfortable again, another note:

YOUR DOG BARKS FOR HOURS ON END, *ALL DAY* AND *ALL NIGHT*. LEAVING YOUR DOG ALONE IS UNFAIR TO YOUR DOG, UNFAIR TO YOUR NEIGBHORS, AND AGAINST THE LAW. FIX IT OR I WILL CALL THE POLICE!!!

Gurl, no. You did not just accuse me of being a bad dog mother.

If the threat to call the police was meant to intimidate me, it had the opposite effect. It snapped me to attention.

Pip couldn't speak for himself, so I would be his defense lawyer. The best defense is a good offense.

A charm offensive.

First, I left a sweet-as-pie reply note on my own door explaining the unfortunate misunderstanding and leaving all my contact info should she wish to discuss it further.

Although I never heard from my accuser, I know she received it, because she ripped the note from my door, leaving a bit of torn tape and paper behind.

Luckily, I retained a copy for my records.

Second, instead of being afraid of my neighbors, I was chatty and solicitous. I held doors, I helped unload groceries, I brought coffee to the doormen. And each time, I was sure to bring up the case of mistaken identity in our conversation.

"I just feel so sorry I can't help whoever is being disturbed, but you know it couldn't be Pip," I'd say.

"Oh, no, I never hear him bark. He's such a good boy."

Say it louder, so the jury can hear you.

I called our superintendent myself and said I had a sensitive matter to discuss. He came over, and I told him, through quavering voice, how upset I was that a mystery neighbor would think I was so inconsiderate and was now leaving threatening notes.

"I mean, 'barking all day'? My Pip?" I gestured to the dog, who lay flat on the ground. He wagged his tail lightly when I said his name.

He couldn't have performed better if I'd coached him.

"If all my tenants were as nice and quiet as you and Pip, my job would be much easier," my super said. "Do you have the note?"

Of course I'd preserved the evidence.

He read it. "I think I know who this might be. Lots of problems with this tenant, not your fault. Don't worry, I'll take care of this."

"Oh, thank you, thank you!" I was relieved. And I was confident that I wouldn't hear from my cranky neighbor again.

I never did.

Turns out, the illuminati is me.

Question Authority

Lisa

History was made in the Supreme Court, this week.

Why?

That's your question, isn't it?

It's a natural question.

And just coincidentally, it's the very point of this column, which is that history was made this week in the Supreme Court because it is the first time in ten years that Justice Clarence Thomas has asked a question.

This would be my kind of Supreme Court Justice.

I'm guessing he never asked a question because he has all the answers.

I mean, what good is a Supreme Court Justice if he has to go asking the lawyers questions every time they come in to argue their case?

He's not there to do *their* job.

He's there to do his job.

Which is to . . . well, be.

In a robe.

You've heard the expression, "Question authority."

Well, you don't need to question authority if you *are* the authority.

You've probably also heard people say, "Can I ask a dumb question?"

And whenever somebody says that, usually somebody else will say something like, "There are no dumb questions."

But Justice Thomas knows that isn't true.

Every question is a dumb question.

Especially if you know everything.

And are smarter than absolutely everyone.

The sheer brilliance of Justice Thomas can be better understood when you realize that only the toughest cases in the entire country reach the lofty heights of the Supreme Court. In fact, I was curious about the percentage of cases that got to the high court, so I went online to the Supreme Court's website to find that information. Of course, the first place I turned was their FAQs, which stands for Frequently Asked Questions.

Justice Thomas never has Frequently Asked Questions.

Only dumb people do, like me.

And others who use websites for information.

The answer on the website says verbatim, "The Court receives approximately 7,000–8,000 petitions for a writ of certiorari each Term. The Court grants and hears oral argument in about 80 cases."

The website didn't say what percentage that is.

But you get the idea.

It's pretty damn few.

And I know from my lawyer days that the Supreme Court takes only those cases that are the most demanding, difficult, and cutting-edge in all of American jurisprudence.

So you can imagine how incredibly brilliant Justice Clarence Thomas is that he doesn't even have a question about these impossibly difficult legal cases that come before him.

I stand in awe.

Because I have questions about everything.

My first question is, if the Supreme Court gets eight thousand petitions and only grants eighty, what percentage is that?

I think the answer is either 10 percent or 1 percent, but I'm bad at decimals.

And I have other questions, too.

In fact, I have so many questions, my head can't hold them all.

And my questions aren't even about the hard cases that come before the Supreme Court, but just about the dumb stuff that happens to me every day.

For example, can I ever train the dogs not to bother the cat?

Or, why do I keep forgetting where I left my phone?

And, who keeps peeing on the rug in the entrance hall?

Is it me?

I can never stay quiet when I have questions and often interrupt people who are saying things, just to start asking questions. For example, if I get lost and you start giving me directions, I will ask you in thirty seconds if you just said left or right. It's not that I didn't hear you, it's just that I have a question.

I have questions about everything I read and about everything I see on TV, and sometimes I even have questions for myself, like why am I watching this dumb TV show?

I'M FULL OF QUESTIONS.

So as soon as I heard that Justice Thomas had asked his first question in ten years, I had a question.

The question was, What was Justice Thomas's question?

So I looked it up and found out that the case involved a man named Mr. Voisine who had shot and killed a bald eagle, and when the police went to Mr. Voisine's house to investigate, they found a gun. But as it turned out, Mr. Voisine had a criminal record of fourteen convictions for domestic violence, and because of that, his owning a rifle was in violation of the Lautenberg Amendment, a federal statute that makes it illegal for convicted domestic abusers to own guns.

Justice Thomas's question was, "Can you give me another area where a misdemeanor violation suspends a constitutional right?"

Which is proof that there are dumb questions.

No matter how you feel about gun rights, I think we can all agree that a man with fourteen counts of domestic abuse, in addition to taking aim at our nation's symbol, is not the poster boy for the NRA.

Justice Stephen Breyer almost said as much, when he replied, "We don't have to decide that here."

And, of course, I have a question.

My question is, What the *hell*?

But lately, that is becoming an FAQ.

Something We Can All Agree On

Lisa

I'm watching everything about the elections.

I'm watching the Republicans.

I'm watching the Democrats.

I'm watching the debates and the rallies.

I'm watching the entrance polls and the exit polls.

You get the idea.

I'm all over the election situation.

Bottom line, there's a lot of dissent and discord.

But I have found the one thing we can all agree on:

We must stop having people sitting or standing behind the candidate while the candidate is speaking.

It's distracting.

I try to listen to what the candidate is saying, keeping my mind open and giving everybody a chance. But there's a slew of random people sitting behind him, and I start watching them instead of the candidate.

Look at that hot guy in the front row.

Does he have a wedding ring?

If not, does he have a pulse?

That's all I ask.

A functioning circulatory system.

Blood pressure.

North and south.

Don't forget south.

I forget why, but it's important.

Or if there's no hot guy, there's a woman behind the candidate, looking down at her phone the *entire* time the candidate is speaking.

Which drives me nuts.

What kind of person sits three feet away from a person who might become the next President of the United States and looks at her phone during the entire speech?

I try to watch the candidate but all I can think of is, what is she doing on that damn phone?

I forgive her only if she's reading a novel.

One of mine.

But I doubt that she is. My readers are geniuses who pay attention when something important is happening, like a speech by the potential LEADER OF THE FREE WORLD.

Plus, I get distracted by the outfits that the people in the background are wearing. I try to size up who they are, what they're like, whether they're like me, and whether they're just slobs.

Full disclosure, I'm just a slob.

Worst of all is when they wear funny costumes, because I'm completely distracted by them. Once when Donald Trump was speaking, behind him was a person dressed exactly like a wall.

I got distracted.

It was a terrific wall outfit.

I'd like to see Wall Guy on Halloween.

What does he wear?

Dockers and a polo?

And then there's the times the candidates are interviewed outside, standing or sitting on director's chairs. Sure as shooting, there's a group of random people behind them, looking motley as all hell.

In fact, "sure as shooting" is a poor choice of words, because that's what distracts me. Every time I see the people who stand so close to a presidential candidate, I worry if they're going to shoot the candidate.

It's not funny, but it's true.

I can't help it.

It's how I think.

I try to watch the candidate during the interview, but instead I end up watching the random people, praying that none of them goes for a weapon.

It makes no sense to let them stand there.

It's an assassination-waiting-to-happen.

Those people don't have to go through a metal detector to stand so close to a candidate because, at this point, the candidates are only candidates. But one minute after the candidate gets elected, they get security.

Until then, all they got is me.

And then during one of the debates, I got distracted by a bunch of kids in the audience, because the houselights were on and the kids made faces, bopped around in their seats, and tried to get on TV.

In other words, they acted like kids.

First, I was annoyed at the kids, but then I started worrying about them.

I knew they were going to get yelled at on the ride home.

Then I worried they were going to be punished by their parents, teased at school, and embarrassed for the rest of their lives, labeled as The Kids Who Acted Out At The Debate.

Don't they know the adults are the only ones allowed to act out at debates?

And then there was the debate where some woman in the audience kept whooping. We couldn't see her, but we could hear her, like the most distracting laugh track ever.

So from now on, let's have the candidates speak in a bubble, with no random people watching, clapping, or wearing wall costumes.

This election is stressful enough.

Topsy-Turvy

Francesca

My best guy friend and I live two blocks away from each other and we share one very particular interest: Gilbert & Sullivan.

William S. Gilbert and Arthur Sullivan were the writer-composer duo that created fourteen comic operas in the late nineteenth century. Their humor is satirical, heavy on wordplay, and pokes fun at Victorian England and theatrical clichés of the day.

Don't make that face. Before *Hamilton* and rap musicals, there were patter-songs.

While others bonded over keg stands in college, my friend and I grew close standing onstage in various G&S productions. So when he found the Gilbert & Sullivan Society of New York on Facebook, we had to go to a meeting.

I remember when we first walked into the church basement where the club meets, someone helpfully asked us if we were lost. (This happened again at the second and third meetings we attended).

We're about fifty years younger than the average member. That didn't stop us. My friend and I were both close to our grandmothers, and we appreciate the value of intergenerational friendship. The members showed us the only authentic, top-notch diner in midtown, and my friend redesigned the group's website to actually make it functional.

The problem is that for nearly a year, we didn't pay any dues, though not for lack of trying.

The first time, the club president said it was a month before the end of their membership year, so he insisted we wait to buy in at the next meeting.

But we didn't go to the very next meeting. We went a few months later and offered again to pay, but the treasurer wasn't there that night, and whomever we spoke to was worried he'd lose track of our twenty bucks.

After that, we felt so guilty for singing for free and mooching the refreshments of Nilla wafers and apple juice, we wouldn't take no for an answer.

The treasurer still resisted. "Well, it's the middle of the season, so I could prorate your dues . . ."

"Don't worry about it, really," I pleaded. "I'm happy to pay, we want to support."

"All right then. And if you both join today, you can save money with a joint membership."

"Sure." Anything to get him to agree and alleviate our guilt.

We paid in cash. Then he told us to fill out a form to get our membership cards and monthly newsletter, The Palace Peeper.

With great pride, he informed us, "We send out a proper paper newsletter—not a virtual one on *the email*."

To be fair, I sound like this when I talk about Snapchat. Time comes for us all.

It was only when we were filling out the form later that I saw there was space for only one address.

"Oh no, I think they think we're married," I said to my friend.

"Nah, you just have to write small."

We looked at each other for a beat, brows furrowed.

I know, what did I think joint membership meant? A platonic, bring-a-friend discount? I can only say our misunderstanding was genuine. I'm so single that married-people-perks don't immediately come to mind.

We certainly never *said* we were a couple.

But then I started thinking . . . we do always attend meetings together.

And after one meeting, in a discussion of cab-sharing with some other members, I said, "We live in the West Village."

I *we*'ed them!

And at the *Mikado* sing-through last summer, they asked how we each came to love Gilbert & Sullivan, I recalled my friend's answer:

"We actually met our freshman year of college in a production of *Pirates of Penzance*. I was a pirate—"

"—and I was a maiden," I chimed in.

"We got paired up for the Act 1 finale dance—"

"—and he almost dropped me!"

"I did, I almost dropped her. But we've been big fans ever since."

We told them our meet-cute.

At that moment, I realized that we had accidentally scammed the Gilbert & Sullivan Society of New York, a group of perfectly lovely senior citizens.

We are so going to hell.

When it's time to renew, I swear, we will definitely spring for two individual memberships. Right now, I'm too embarrassed to correct them.

Someday, we'll break it to them that we were never a couple and we won't be giving birth to the next generation of modern, major, millennials.

Maybe when they're older.

Adventures in Herpetology

Lisa

I have a new boyfriend.

Unfortunately, he's a snake in the grass.

Literally, not figuratively.

I divorced my figurative snakes.

Let me explain.

Spring has sprung, and last week on St. Patrick's Day, I went out to my garden. I hadn't done any gardening yet, which if you recall from last season, is not my forte.

I started a perennial garden that's perennially horrible.

My problem seems to be one of excess, in that I do too much of everything. I don't water plants, I waterboard plants.

But hope springs eternal, just like weeds, and I went out to my garden last week to start all over again. The garden is right outside my front door, divided in two sides by my front walk, and it was mostly brown after winter. But it was green in spots, and I went into the garden and started to look really closely, to see if anything was growing.

I thought I saw something moving, but I figured it was my imagination.

So I looked closer.

It wasn't. It was a little green tip of something, sticking out from under a rock, and on impulse, I moved the rock.

And freaked the hell out.

Because right before me was a writhing mass of full-grown snakes.

I ran screaming back into the house.

By the way, recall that it was St. Patrick's Day and the legend of St. Patrick is that he drove the snakes from Ireland.

Evidently, he drove them into my garden, where they have taken up residence.

I stood inside the house, shuddering and watching the spot where the snakes had been, but it was hard to see them from a distance. I couldn't tell what kind of snakes they were, which worried me. If they were garter snakes, I could pretend that none of this had happened and go about my life.

Of course, I was doubting that I would ever garden again.

Or even walk to my front door.

Not to mention that I've been thinking about adding a little room onto the front of my house that I've been calling the garden room, so that I could see the garden from the kitchen.

Now I wasn't sure I wanted to see the garden.

Ever again.

But if the snakes were poisonous, then I supposed I would have to call an exterminator, which I didn't want to do. I like living things too much to kill them, even a snake.

That's just how I feel about animals.

There are, however, a few people who remain excellent candidates for homicide.

But I hear that's against the law.

To return to point, I got my courage up, went back outside, and stood at a safe distance to see what the snakes were up to. They were all gone except for one, slithering on top of the stone wall around the garden.

At first he gave me the creeps, but the more I looked at him, the less scared I got of him. He was green and black, so I figured he was a garter snake and he wouldn't try to kill me, so I wasn't going to kill him. Then I took pictures and videos of him, and in short order, he became the most photographed snake in the world.

If you don't count certain politicians.

Take your pick.

My lips are sealed.

Actually, they're sssssssseealed.

To make a long story short, I spent a lot of time watching that snake, and the next thing I knew, he was actually watching me.

I'm not kidding.

His face was turned in my direction, and his dark eyes looked at me directly, or as directly as they could, given that one eye is on the left side of his head and the other's on the right.

It's not an attractive look for anybody but a snake.

Plus he had a little red forked tongue, which he flicked in and out.

Sexy.

I mean, this was the Bradley Cooper of snakes.

And you know what?

I'm going to keep him.

And in the end, maybe I turned out to be a great gardener.

Because I grew snakes.

The Scent of a Woman

Lisa

Did you hear about the new dating service?

It works by smell.

In other words, it stinks.

Literally.

It's called "smell dating" and has a website all its own, which has a very large picture of nostrils.

I'm not kidding.

Don't turn your nose up.

In fact, it's probably no worse a way to find a mate than the ways I found them, which led to Thing One and Thing Two.

And two divorces.

As I've said, I don't regret the divorces.

I regret the marriages.

I didn't notice the smell.

But the flies did.

Anyway, to stay on point, there is actually a new thing called smell dating, which advertises itself as "the first mail odor dating service."

Get it?

And how it works is that you send the company twenty-five dollars and they send you a shirt to wear for three days and three nights, without deodorant.

So far, so good.

I have twenty-five dollars and I have been known to not change my shirt for three days and three nights.

In fact, while we're oversharing, I don't wear deodorant anymore. Call me crazy but I don't want to smear aluminum chlorohydrate, parabens, propylene glycol, triclosan, triethanolamine, and diethanolamine on my armpits.

I save that stuff for my breasts.

Just kidding.

God intended me to sweat, and I like it that way.

Lucky for me, everyone I live with feels the exact same way.

Oh, wait.

I forgot.

I live alone.

There is no relationship between these facts.

It's not my smell that compels my solitude.

It's my choice.

Or maybe it's my personality, but that's neither here nor there.

I know I'm not the only woman who doesn't want to wear deodorant because I noticed that there's a new company that has sprung up to market a natural deodorant made of charcoal.

I've yet to do this. I'm not sure that smearing charcoal on my underarm is an improvement on perspiration.

But it will come in handy in time for summer barbecuing.

The truth is, I hardly sweat because I sit on my butt all day long and the only part of me that moves is my fingers.

And when I do sweat, it smells like rainbows and rose petals.

I know this because the dogs told me.

Anyway, to stay on point, I always keep an eye out for news stories to report to you, and the smell-dating story caught my eye.

And my nose.

The way smell dating works is that after wearing the T-shirt, you return it to the company in a prepaid envelope and they send you ten swatches from T-shirts worn by other people, for three days and three nights without deodorant.

Yes, you read that correctly.

People are mailing their dirty laundry to each other.

I'm hoping for the dating service that allows me to mail the company my dirty shirts, and they will wash them and send them back to me.

Now if there was a guy who I could do that with, I would date him.

But again, not how it works.

After you smell the samples, you're supposed to tell the company which sample you like.

I know which sample I like.

The guy who smells like chocolate cake.

If someone whose smell you like happens to like your smell, then the company will allow you to exchange contact information and you can meet each other.

At a bar.

Of soap.

I made that last part up.

I don't know if smell dating is a worse idea than any other, and I was curious about the research, so I turned to the website

FAQ section and read the question: "I'm looking for a serious relationship, is this service for me?'

Here is the answer:

"The olfactory apparatus is a nontrivial source of information and the extent of its impact on our social lives is currently unknown."

Would you like me to translate?

"We have no idea."

In other words, there may be no point to smell dating, at all.

If you're cynical, like some people we know (not me) (okay, me), you might think that the point would be the twenty-five dollars. After all, there might be enough smelly people who are also dumb enough to part with twenty-five dollars in order to get shreds of somebody else's dirty laundry, in the vain hope of finding love, happiness, and joy.

Or Cheer.

But surprisingly, the company claims to be not-for-profit, and that its "finances are available upon request."

Should we request?

I think so.

Because something smells fishy.

Pay the Troll

Francesca

To care about politics in the age of social media is to be a little angry all the time.

If the twenty-four-hour cable news cycle wasn't enough, Twitter and Facebook will help you find something new and enraging to click on 86,400 seconds a day.

This primary election has been brutal. Even if you have a candidate you're passionate about, especially if you do, the Internet can be toxic.

Toxic yet alluring. Why is it so much more tempting to click on an article with a headline you abhor than one that you agree with?

Lab mice are smarter than that.

But I do it. I don't generate many political posts myself, but I consume them, ravenously. And as a writer, I do enough stress-eating in front of the computer.

Online rage isn't cathartic, like yelling at a bad call on the football field, or "gesturing" at the cab that almost hit you in the crosswalk. You experience it alone, in silence, while holding a small, fragile, electronic device.

A smartphone doesn't have the heft of a pitchfork.

Not that pitchforks belong in politics, but it seems many social media users are more interested in generating virtual angry mobs than productive political discourse, much less revolution.

You can't march in a straight line while looking down at your phone.

The agita was getting to me, so I tried to reduce my Internet-induced bile.

First, whenever I would see a political post that got my blood pumping, I'd recenter and pay it forward by retweeting a GIF of a kitten falling asleep, or a puppy doing a somersault, or any cute baby animal image I could find.

The Internet's greatest achievement is its catalogue of cute.

Yeah, yeah, also the worldwide information exchange— but have you *seen* the GIF of the baby sloth handing a person a flower? It's special.

But cute couldn't compete with the production line of click-bait hot takes and insulting memes.

I tried "muting" or "unfollowing" those users who vehemently disagreed with me and following many more who shared my views, so that I could live in a peaceful bubble of validation.

Yes, this is intellectually dissatisfying and goes against my belief in the value of varied opinions. But I might have stuck with it to get through this election, if only it had worked.

Many of the strangers I agreed with online mainly wanted to vent their own rage to a receptive audience. They shared the most preposterous articles in order to point out the bias and falsehoods, and they retweeted the most offensive trolls to showcase their snarky retorts.

The camaraderie of feeling in the trenches together came at the cost of feeling even more under siege.

Echo chambers are still loud.

I'm not interested in being right and proving others wrong. Political discussion has become so polarized, even within parties, that you can feel like you're hated for your views—and that hurts.

Or it infuriates.

Then I had a novel idea: get off-line.

My candidate was having a rally, and I decided to go by myself. I felt dorky and exposed, unused to having my political views out in the sunlight. But as I waited in line, I struck up a conversation with a fellow supporter. We gushed about our candidate, but also discussed how her brother supports the opponent. No one was angry about it.

I was so moved by the positivity at the rally, I signed up to phone bank. Calling strangers is awkward, but when you're talking human to human, even dissenters are pretty polite. And some of the supporters were so excited to get to the polls, despite hardships like caring for a sick spouse, or wrangling two kids under age six, or standing in line after a twelve-hour shift, I'd hang up the phone misty-eyed.

I graduated to canvassing. Approaching strangers on the street goes against my training as a New Yorker, but after one tough day, I brought along the best icebreaker: my dog. I crafted him a bandana with the campaign logo (the dork-ship has sailed) and had a great day talking to supporters.

Volunteering has made me more invested in my candidate, and yet, I feel . . . happy?

I'm reminded that politics is about community: people joining together to try to come up with the best answers to tough questions and the best ways to take care of each other.

I prefer politics in person.

Ball o' Fun

Lisa

There's a girl at my house having an orgy.

But it's not me.

It's my Susan The Snake, who lives in my garden with thirty of her new boyfriends.

In fact, I just caught them having sssssssssex.

I'm not making this up.

Let me explain, because in all of my years writing about my misadventures in this house, this one is the most incredible.

You will recall that I wrote previously about a garter snake that I discovered in my garden. I thought she was cute, and once I got over the initial heebie-jeebies, I liked having her around. I even took pictures and movies of her, because I thought she was interesting. I named her, like an idiot.

Well, those days are over.

Because I happened to walk down my front walk today and suddenly, on the flagstone landing was something I had never seen before in my entire life—a massive moving ball of live snakes, writhing all over each other.

No, I wasn't drinking.

But I am now.

I jumped back, screaming, and all of a sudden the snakes went in a million different directions, which was even scarier. I had no idea that snakes could move that fast, and they fled immediately for holes around the garden that I didn't even know existed.

I ran into the house, and Francesca happened to be home, so I did what any respectable mother would do.

I fled into the arms of my daughter.

Francesca gave me a hug, listened to my story, then we grabbed her phone to make a video. We both went outside, where she was much braver than I, so she filmed the snakes breaking up their snake ball. She thought the entire episode was incredibly cool.

I did not.

Instead, I went online to try to understand what I had seen, because that's the way things are nowadays, wherein we require electronic means to understand Nature.

All I had to do was Google "garter snake ball."

Well, you guessed it.

The snakes were having a ball.

Literally.

This mass of mating snakes is called a "mating ball."

Apparently I had witnessed the mating ritual of garter snakes, a sight that will turn your stomach or make you jealous, depending on how single a girl you are.

I'm not that single.

The bottom line is this time of year, a female snake will come out of hibernation and give off pheromones to attract male snakes. Dozens of male snakes will pick up the scent and attempt to mate with one female. One article said that a matting ball has "up to 25 males per female," but another article said that the males mate with a single female "in droves."

So Susan gets around.

I hate to slut-shame a snake, but still.

Sssssslut.

One article said that a single female will attract so many snakes that "homeowners sometimes think garter snakes are overrunning their neighborhoods."

Great.

I am that homeowner.

But I don't think the snakes are overrunning my neighborhood. I think they're overrunning my garden.

But wait, it gets worse.

Garter snakes bear live young, and they give birth to seven to eighty-seven baby snakes.

WHAT?

I'm going to have eighty-seven snakes in my front yard? To add to the snake that I already have?

Not only that, but I researched further and found out that the gestational period for garter snakes is two to three months, so I'm looking forward to a sssssssssssummer of ssssssssssnakes.

But then I read more, and it turns out that the female garter snakes are able to store sperm in their body and fertilize themselves at will.

This is good news for the female garter snake.

But bad news for me.

I'm looking forward to a rolling tide of baby garter snakes as long as Susan decides she likes kids.

I have no idea what to do about this.

My reaction got only so far as to write about it, so you can share my horror.

Because that's what friends are for.

My only other thought was how fast can I get a sign at the curb:

FOR SSSSSSSSSALE.

Going Where the Weather Suits My Clothes

Lisa

I have yoga pants, so sooner or later, it was bound to happen.

I went to a yoga class.

And I lived.

Barely.

It came about because my friend Nan had started going to yoga, then my friend Paula started going, then all of a sudden every other middle-aged woman I know, all of whom had yoga pants, started going to yoga.

Yoga pants are the gateway drug to actual yoga.

I don't even remember why I got yoga pants in the first place.

I suspect it had something to do with the elastic waistband.

Anyway, everybody I know was raving about yoga, and I was feeling very achy and blobby after winter, so I decided to join Nan at her beginner class on Saturday morning.

I figured, how hard can it be?

I got dressed in my yoga pants, but then I realized I had

no yoga shirt, or basically anything that fits close enough so that when you go upside down it will not reveal your elastic waistband.

Or your elastic waist.

But I'm getting ahead of myself.

I got to the class early because that's how I am on the first day of school.

I felt vaguely nervous waiting for everyone in the woo-woo yoga studio, which had a lot of stuff for sale.

Maybe shopping was the warm-up.

Unfortunately, the only things they sold were crystals, worry beads, and gluten-and-dairy-free candy bars.

By which I mean, candy bars without the candy.

Also I don't need beads to worry.

I can worry without accessories.

I'm a professional worrier.

It comes with the ovaries.

Evidently, new-age gifts don't appeal to me, in my old age.

There was only one thing for sale that tempted me, and it was called Be Happy Mist. It was a small spray bottle of clear fluid that claimed to "restore peace, ease suffering, and clear negative emotions."

The sign said, "Do you want to be happier?"

I thought it was a trick question.

It's hard to imagine you could be any happier than wearing a pair of pants with no waistband.

It was also safe for "adults, children, pets, and plants."

Which is quite something.

I don't think it's possible to restore peace among my pets.

And my plants come with negative emotions.

Because my garden is growing snakes.

So I didn't buy anything while I waited for the teacher to arrive, but in time she did and so did Nan, and we introduced ourselves, went to a pretty room, and immediately started what is called the "practice."

Unfortunately, I should have practiced for the practice.

The very first thing we did was lie down on a mat on our back, reach our hands over our heads, and try to curve our bodies into the shape of a C, to the right and to the left.

Which was impossible.

The most I got was a backslash.

I couldn't make a C on either side, and at one point while I was trying, I actually fell down, which is incredible because I was already on the floor.

Ten minutes later, we had gone through an array of poses, or stretching exercises, and I couldn't do any of them. I was sweating, burping, and cursing.

In my mind.

Profanity is unwelcome in a yoga studio.

Also farting.

I held it in.

Correction, *them* in.

Really, all that squeezing toned my butt.

Maybe that's how yoga works?

My muscles wiggled if I tried to hold a position, and the instructor said you were supposed to time your breathing to the stretching, which was when I realized I was holding my breath, probably trying to pass out so they would call 911 and rescue me from class.

All the poses had names, like Downward Dog, which was

named by someone who never met a dog, since all of mine are Upward Dogs.

And when we came to Happy Baby pose, I wanted to give up because I felt like such an Unhappy Baby.

But I stayed with it, and when class was over, I noticed my back had stopped hurting.

My ego was bruised, but that's nothing new.

So I'm going back for a second class.

Namaste.

Brain Freeze

Francesca

I'm being gaslighted by my refrigerator.

For months, I'd been suspicious of my freezer, specifically that it's thawing and refreezing my food. A bag of frozen peas, once loose and flexible, is transmuted into a solid block of bumpy ice by the time I go to cook them. No matter how many times I've sneaked "just a spoonful" from a pint of ice cream—yes, living alone rules—the ice cream's surface will be rendered smooth and flat, the evidence of my nibbling erased.

"Maybe I didn't break my diet after all," I'd say to myself the next night I opened the container.

Add "enabler" to my list of grievances.

But I procrastinated on calling an appliance-repair company. After all, I wasn't completely sure it was broken.

Until I went on vacation. Upon return, I opened the fridge and was hit with a putrid stench. The interior of the fridge was balmy, and the food inside looked like a science experiment.

Through the nausea, I felt validated.

The repairman who examined it said the 'temperature regulator' needed to be replaced. I explained my prior concerns about the freezer, and he said it was likely the cause of that, too. I paid for the service and the new part.

But a few weeks later, my freezer was slowing down again—this time I was certain. My shrinking ice cubes looked like the victim of global warming, missing only a tiny polar bear waving a white flag.

Even my bag of Ezekiel bread was sweating like a whore in church.

Thankfully, the repair service had a ninety-day guarantee, and this was less than a month later. I called, and they sent out a different repairman.

I caught the new guy up to speed. He opened the freezer.

"Feels cold to me."

You pay extra for the expertise.

"It's cold *now,* but it's not maintaining a freezing temperature. Look, I'm not crazy." I brought out Exhibit A, a box of fruit pops, and showed him how each popsicle was a wonky shape, half off its stick, its cellophane bag filled with red goo.

He pinched the popsicle between his fingers. "That's frozen."

"But look at it. It clearly melted at some point."

"They could have been like that when you bought them."

"No, they were fine before."

"How could I know that for sure?"

"Because . . . I'm telling you. It's the reason I knew something was wrong. It's why I called you." I was so bewildered by his skepticism, I actually laughed. "Do you think I'm lying?"

He smirked and shrugged, like that was a definite possibility.

Women, am I right? Always crying wolf for refrigerator-attention.

It was like I had slipped down a wormhole of retro gender dynamics. I stood barefoot and helpless in my kitchen while a man patronizingly explained how I don't know what I know.

"A freezer cycles to maintain its temperature. That's how a thermostat works."

Dude, don't mansplain cycles to a woman.

"Cycles to the point where things melt? I swear, it's malfunctioning. This happened before the fridge broke down a few weeks ago, and it's doing it again. Can you think what might cause that?"

He threw up his hands. Then he began writing something on his clipboard.

At this point the only thing icing over was me. "So you don't know how to fix it."

"I can't fix something that isn't broken." He tore off a sheet and handed it to me. It was a bill.

I explained that this was still under the last repair's warranty.

"The warranty is for the repair, not the service call."

"Right, but the last repair didn't work. My fridge is broken again, hence this service call."

"Only the part we replaced is guaranteed, it still works."

Ah yes, the 'temperature regulator.' Works like a charm.

But this was bizarro-world, where up is down and hot is cold.

I handed over my credit card so I could get this guy out of my apartment and return to sanity.

The truth is, the fridge is nearly fifteen years old, I don't want to put any more money into it. I've decided I'm going to buy a new one entirely.

Soon.

I've continued to live with my freezer, convinced it's not safe to eat anything from, but reluctant to pull the trigger on buying a new one. Why?

Now it's in my head—what if I *am* crazy?

Leave a Tip

Lisa

There's a new restaurant in London and you go there to eat naked.

I'm not making this up.

This restaurant hasn't even opened yet but it's already getting major attention, and not for the food. I went to the restaurant's website and it didn't even have a menu posted.

Food isn't the point, would be my guess.

Like nobody complains about the plot in porn. Even though there's never a twist and the ending is always happy.

Step up your game, pornographers.

You might think you would never go to a naked restaurant, but it has a waiting list of thirty thousand.

I'm not exaggerating, for once.

The restaurant is called The Bunyadi, and I'm not sure what a bunyadi is, but let's pretend it's something usually covered by your underwear.

So this is a restaurant where you bring your own bunyadi. B.Y.O.B.

And you and your bunyadi eat completely naked, in an area the restaurant calls "pure."

I would call it "hairy," "smelly," and "vaguely unsanitary."
But that's just me.

There's also a "non-naked" section, where the stiffs sit.

Or presumably, the less stiff.

I don't know, it's kind of confusing.

I think you're allowed to put your napkin in your lap.

In fact, you'd better.

Still, I would never go to a naked restaurant. I don't want anyone to see me eating naked. In fact, I don't want anybody to see me sitting down naked. I own an entire wardrobe of shirts and sweaters to hide what I really look like when I sit down, because of my rolls.

If I ate at a naked restaurant, I'd have to hide my rolls behind the rolls.

In fact, my rolls are the first thing I'd want to hide, not my breasts or my bunyadi.

I bet I'm not alone in this, as a middle-aged woman.

Am I right, sisters?

Aren't our rolls keeping Chico's in business?

If every girl's best friend is an elastic waistband, every girl's other best friend is the insanely blousy shirt that goes over it to hide our rolls.

I've seen it called Goddesswear, which is as good a euphemism as any.

It's really clothes for women who have better things to do than sit-ups.

Me.

I shudder to imagine a world where all the restaurants turn naked.

It would be a disaster for middle-aged women.

All of a sudden, we'd start cooking like fiends.

Like we used to when we were feeding families or had something to prove.

Back when we cared.

Do you remember those days?

I don't.

Maybe the way you feel about a naked restaurant depends on whether you have an awesome body or not.

And if you remember the days of the smoking section, you're probably not in the smoking-hot section.

Naked restaurants would be a disaster for middle-aged men too, but men are never ashamed of their bodies, even when they should be.

Just saying, gentlemen.

It's a scientific fact that mirrors don't work for men.

Or on the contrary, maybe they do.

Because a man will look at a mirror and think he looks great, no matter what he looks like, and a woman will look in a mirror and think she looks terrible, no matter what she looks like.

So clearly, the problem is mirrors.

What are they up to?

Anyway, to stay on point, I wouldn't go to a naked restaurant because I don't want to see anyone eating naked.

Nobody looks good when they're eating, whether their bunyadi is showing or not.

The proof is on CNN. Political candidates look dumb when they eat, and even though Hillary Clinton declined to eat in front of the cameras in New York, she couldn't stop eyeing the cheesecake.

That would be me.

It's not nudity that turns me on, it's food.

In other words, my cheesecake is cheesecake.

Scrambled Eggs

Lisa

The hits just keep on coming at the Scottoline farm, where the animals outnumber the people.

They like it that way.

I don't, especially when I wonder who's running the joint. The only thing I'm sure of is who's paying the bills.

Right now the chickens are in charge.

Because bottom line, they're not producing any eggs.

Neither am I, but that's another subject. No one's counting on me for breakfast.

The chickens have no excuse. They still have estrogen.

By the way, my chickens might not be laying eggs, but my snakes are.

Ssssssensational.

In fact, just today I found a molted snakeskin in the garden.

Don't you hate it when your snakes leave their clothes around?

To return to the story, one day my chickens stopped laying eggs, which bugged me.

Ingrates.

They have it great, in that they're a small flock of fifteen and they live in a big wooden coop.

For free.

They also have a large outdoor run, so they can exercise.

Like a gym that you actually use.

Also, it takes work to keep chickens, in that their coop has to be cleaned, and they have to be fed and given fresh water, so the least they could do is squeeze out an egg or two every day, like they used to before they started slacking.

By the way, don't get the idea that I do all the work for the chickens, because I hire someone to do that, as I am too busy and/or lazy, and if you think it's easy to pay people to do all the work you are too busy/lazy to do, you need to think again.

Slackers!

But then one day, I went to the coop, noticed some broken eggshells, and realized that the chickens were laying eggs—but eating them themselves.

They were the Hannibal Lecters of chickens.

Hennibal Lechters!

This had never happened before, and I had no idea what to do about it. I started checking the coop twice a day, trying to beat the chickens to the eggs, but they won every time.

I can't outsmart a chicken.

Still wanna read my books?

I did some research online, and it said that chickens could develop a habit of eating their own eggs and the only way to break them of it was by mixing some eggs with Tabasco sauce, pouring the eggs back into an eggshell, and returning it to the henhouse.

So I did that.

Yes, I made eggs for chickens.

I made food for what other people think is food.

Plus I delivered it to them like room service.

Remind me again who's ruling the roost.

Anyway, it didn't work. The chickens ate even more eggs, and I got the distinct impression that they would've also enjoyed a side of home fries, buttered wheat toast, and a cup of hot coffee.

I went back to the Internet, where it said you could also try training them not to eat their eggs by replacing their eggs with golf balls.

Fore!

So I dug up some of my golf balls from last year's lessons and put them in the coop, but the next thing that happened was that the hens began fighting over which one got to sit on the golf balls.

News flash, chickens like club sports.

The hens sat on the golf balls all day long, and I couldn't get the balls from them without being pecked, and when I succeeded, the balls were so hot they were practically hard-boiled.

Yum. Cooked Titleist.

Yet again, I went back to the Internet and found out that you could buy a fake wooden egg that was guaranteed to train chickens out of eating their own eggs, so I ordered a few.

And it worked!

Today my fake egg yielded a real egg.

Evidently, I tricked my chickens.

That makes me the trickiest chick of all.

 Anniversary

Francesca

Exactly one year ago, I was assaulted in my neighborhood.

It's not the sort of anniversary you want to celebrate, but one you can't help but remember.

During the attack, I believed the stranger could kill me. Thankfully, I escaped only badly beaten and robbed. My assailant was never caught.

In the months following, I dealt with some of the typical posttraumatic psychological issues. But my most lingering fear wasn't that I would be attacked again.

I was afraid of becoming a different person.

I liked myself before the assault, and I was afraid of becoming a fearful person, damaged, weak.

Now a year has passed, and I am a different person.

I'm a better person.

I have a greater love and compassion for myself. I was confronted with my human frailty—the parts that bruise and the wounds that can't be seen. But what I feared would break me didn't, and it gave me a greater belief in my own strength and resilience.

I have greater empathy. I am kinder to strangers. I know bad things happen, and I don't assume the person next to me is immune.

I even have empathy for the person who was so desperate and misguided that he resorted to violent crime for extra cash. I've forgiven my attacker. His world is undoubtedly uglier and more frightful than I could ever imagine.

And I have a greater love for my neighborhood. I still live on the street where my blood stained the sidewalk, but I'd never consider moving. One could call that cognitive dissonance, but I disagree. Yes, this is the place where I was hurt, but more important, this is the place where I was healed.

My neighbors aren't just the people who live next door, they're the people who called the police, or who walked their dogs with me at the same time of evening. They're the doormen of other people's buildings who wave to me every night. They're the ones who made me feel happy and safe again.

And yes, I do live with more fear. I was humbled by it, and as a result, I'm less trusting of strangers and more vigilant of my surroundings.

But that doesn't take away the rest. My fear does not eclipse my strength, or my empathy, or my love of my neighbors. Despite the darkness I know exists, I find daily joy and light in the world. That the two coexist makes the goodness even sweeter.

Still, I had my eye on the calendar, wary of any unexpected emotions that might rear up as I approached that anniversary of violence.

Then, just one week shy of my one-year mark, I was stunned

and horrified along with the rest of our nation when a far more heinous act of violence exploded in an Orlando nightclub and into our collective consciousness.

This was brutality on a terrifying scale. A massacre. The worst terrorist attack since 9/11. A hate crime. It was every horrible form of hatred, bigotry, and obscene violence at once.

Watching its aftermath, we witnessed trauma on a national stage. The profound trauma of the victims rippled outward to their loved ones, friends and family, coworkers, acquaintances, the LGBTQ community, allies, Floridians, Americans, and beyond.

Now, we are grieving. So many innocent and beloved people's lives were stolen and cannot be replaced. There is no salve for the pain of their loss, no silver lining to this tragedy, and no easy takeaway message. We can only try to comfort each other.

I attended a vigil for the Orlando victims outside of the civil-rights landmark, The Stonewall Inn. Gay people are some of my best friends and family, and I wanted to pay my respects to the lives lost and the LGBTQ community at large. Stonewall is in my neighborhood. These people are my neighbors. We are a community.

The enormous crowd stretched down Christopher Street and across Seventh Avenue. Many held signs with expressions of love and tolerance. The speakers talked of connection and unity. Together we mourned as the names of the forty-nine victims were read. It was heartbreaking and beautiful and powerful.

I'll never forget it.

Claim love

But a year from now, when the date stands out in our mind, a blot on the calendar, I wonder, how will we be different?

How will we as a country, as a community of Americans, be changed?

The fear is real. Trauma will leave its mark. But it doesn't have to change us for the worse. We can be weathered but not hardened.

I hope we can come together to protect and heal those

in pain, to prove the resilience of our American values of freedom, equality, and tolerance, and to grow in love and empathy.

A year from now, let's be the country where we were healed.

Batter Up!

Lisa

It was last summer that I got major news.

Specifically, it was major-league news.

I'm was going to throw out the first pitch at a Phillies game.

The game was on August 20, when the Phillies played the Cardinals, which was Ladies' Night. Francesca and I were both there, meeting and greeting Ladies before I feared I'd make a fool of myself in front of both genders.

(As you read this, it has happened already, but let me continue as if it hasn't, to give you that you-are-there feeling. Because I WAS THERE!)

It was the day that baseball changed forever.

How often do you think varicose veins show up on the pitcher's mound?

Exactly.

This is Virgin Varicose Territory.

Before I explain how this amazing event came about, let me first state the obvious. This is a huge honor for a hometown girl like me, and I'm very grateful to the Phillies. When I first got the news, my instant reaction was incredible excitement, and my second reaction was:

What do I wear?

Well, it's Ladies' Night, and I think like a Lady.

But also I think like a Middle-Aged Lady who realizes that it's hot in August and that means I can't wear my fleece sweatshirt and fleece sweatpants, which Francesca affectionately calls my teddy-bear clothes.

And that means that I have to wear shorts, displaying to advantage my thigh cellulite, wrinkly knees, and aforementioned varicose veins, running up and down my legs like I-95.

At some point, we Ladies become Google Maps.

I am now Driving Directions.

The only good thing is that the game isn't until August 20, which gives me more than enough time to lose fifty pounds.

Or maybe five.

Or one.

Plus, I have to learn to pitch by then.

No problem.

I looked it up, and the distance from the pitcher's mound to home plate is sixty feet six inches, so I'm pretty sure that I can get the ball over the plate if I stand six inches away.

I want to make a good showing for Ladies everywhere, so when I got the news that this was actually happening, I did the first thing most Ladies would do.

Go shopping.

In order to practice my pitch, I needed a ball and a baseball mitt, though at one point in my life I had both. But my ball and baseball mitt went the way of my sanitary belt, and probably for the same reason:

Who needs it?

So I went out to the store to buy a ball and a baseball mitt, where I was the only sixty-year-old in the aisle trying on baseball gloves.

I picked out a black mitt because it's slimming.

Also it was a Ladies' mitt because it has pink laces.

Actually, I don't think that's sexist, or even if it is, it's not the end of the world, because pink is my favorite color.

You know the joke, there are two times in a woman's life when she likes pink—the first time is when she's six years old and the second time is when she's in menopause.

Wrong on both counts, pink haters.

For me, menopause is a memory.

And now I don't remember.

It's like sex, that way.

To return to point, I didn't have to buy a jersey, or T-shirt, or whatever you call the thing that baseball players wear on top because the Phillies are actually providing me a Phillies baseball jersey that will have my own name on the back.

How cool is that?

Ladies love personalized items.

Just ask Frontgate.

By the way, the Phillies asked me what number I wanted on the back of my jersey. I instantly thought 60, for obvious reasons, but the numbers don't go that high.

Also I didn't want to advertise my waist size.

LOL.

So then I chose number 1, because all Middle-Aged Ladies should be number 1 in their own mind, even if we are number 293874646828238 in the world's mind.

But number 1 was already taken.

Probably by some egomaniac.

So I chose 2.
I try harder.
And I always will.
See you at the game, Ladies.
And thanks, Phillies!

Diaper Genie

Lisa

I just bought diapers.

For Ruby The Crazy Corgi.

Before I explain, let me warn you. If you're squeamish, stop reading now. Go read something else.

Preferably one of our other books.

Or enjoy life some other way.

It's up to you.

This is America.

Just don't say I didn't warn you, if you're truly squeamish about things like poop and peepee.

By the way, before we even begin, let me mention something about things scatological.

(That's an SAT word for poop and peepee, in case you didn't know. I wanted to save you the trouble of looking it up. Because I want to make your life easier. I *care*, people.)

I honestly don't understand why people get squeamish about bodily functions, and I will say now, even though men might write me nasty emails, that I think this is gender-related. Because I have never known a woman to be *that* squeamish about poop and peepee, undoubtedly because we started changing diapers first. I know that men change diapers, too, but I bet they come to it after the seal's broken, and by that point, they know they're not allowed to express their squeamishness or they will get yelled at.

And then, in time, they get cured.

The cure for squeamishness is Get Over Yourself.

And nothing teaches Get-Over-Yourself faster than being a parent.

Anyway, if having a baby doesn't cure you of squeamishness, a dog or cat will. If you own a pet, or a pet owns you, you will get up close and personal with poop, peepee, and whatever glop they're hocking up on your rug, bed, or foot.

So what's happening with Ruby is that, as she got older, she developed degenerative myelopathy, a back disorder that paralyzed her hind end. She uses a doggie cart to get around, and she's otherwise happy and healthy. The vet told me the odds were that she would not become incontinent.

Proof that you should not take me to a casino.

Especially if you're going to play craps.

Because I've been knee deep in the stuff, cleaning up when Ruby poops and pees on rugs, floors, and even her doggie cart.

What's a mother to do?

I tried to anticipate when she would go to the bathroom and I put her outside in the backyard at those times, but that didn't work. A dog's poop schedule is as predictable as a presidential primary election.

Not that these two things are related.

End of political discussion.

I went to the pet store and got special diapers they make

for dogs, but the small-dog-size diaper was too small. Corgis may have short legs, but they're bootylicious.

I returned to the store and got the bigger size, and though it fit her butt, it was too big to use with her cart.

Ruby is the Goldilocks of paralyzed dogs.

Also, the tape strips on the doggie diapers weren't very adhesive. They may have been strong enough for a chihuahua, but for a corgi, you need duct tape.

Don't think I didn't try that.

You haven't lived until you've duct-taped a diaper on a dog.

The problem was that she required three diaper changes a day, necessitating a new duct-taping every time, and you may recall that I have a full-time job.

Those books you should be reading aren't going to write themselves.

So then I decided to try regular baby diapers, but before I went to the store, I went online to the Pampers website to get an idea for sizing. The webpage said, "Need help finding your baby's size? Tell us his age, size, and weight!"

Unfortunately, there was no setting for a twelve-year-old handicapped corgi.

I couldn't even understand from the website which sizes the Pampers came in, except that there were flashy new lines named Cruiser and Swaddler.

I was looking for Pooper.

But they didn't have them, either.

So I went to the store, where, long story short, I gave up on the Pampers altogether and went for the Depends because they didn't have any tape and seemed like they'd fit Ruby better.

I bought them in the self-checkout.

I didn't want to hear myself say to a cashier, "They're not for me, they're for my dog."

Then I took them home and put them on her, easy as pie.

Did they work?

It depends.

So far, so good.

But don't call them diapers, call them adult underwear.

Or adult dog underwear.

Princess Ruby and her royal carriage

And they have Fit-Flex, so they "move with you"—or your corgi.

They're a "neutral peach color," which matches Ruby's fur.

And they fit in her doggie cart.

So we're rolling.

Problem solved.

And whatever adult underwear is left over, I know I'll use myself.

Someday.

Or when I sneeze.

One-Piece of Mind

Francesca

My friend invited me to her birthday at Rockaway beach in May, but I didn't exactly have my summer body back yet.

That usually takes until Labor Day.

So I had disproportionate what-to-wear anxiety. In my bedroom, I tried on every bikini I owned. None fit me the way I liked.

Or as it always is with bathing suits, I didn't fit them the way I like.

Whether I had actually gained weight or it was all in my head, the effect was the same: dread.

Like most women, I've always had a complicated relationship with two-piece suits.

When I was a preteen, I was dying for a bikini. I hassled my mom constantly to let me get one. One-pieces were for little girls, and I wanted to be grown-up.

When I turned thirteen, I got one. It was white and had little embroidered yellow daisies along the edges. I absolutely loved it.

I just didn't love it on me.

That bathing suit did not transform me into the gorgeous sixteen-year-old I wanted to be. Instead, it showed me I had a little potbelly and not-quite-there breasts.

My body confidence has gone up and down since then, but two things have remained true:

I've never felt 100 percent great in a bikini, but I never went back to the one-piece.

Wearing a one-piece has always struck me as an admission of defeat. A capitulation to the notion that only certain bodies are "bikini-ready."

Anybody who wants to wear a bikini is bikini-ready, damn it!

At the same time, maybe wearing a revealing two-piece is capitulating to sexual objectification. I don't have to serve myself up on a platter to every man with eyes. They have to earn it!

But what if the reason I want to wear a one-piece is because I feel bad about my belly?

Not exactly stickin' it to the patriarchy.

I'm so confused how to be a feminist at the beach.

We live at a particularly excruciating moment of feminism, where as young women, we are aware of a more progressive stance on body positivity, yet we were raised in and still live in a sexist society.

It's not easy to hit the eject button on deeply ingrained beauty norms.

What if I'm a feminist who wants to look hot?

What if I'm body-positive but still struggle with body-confidence?

How do you snooze on the beach when you're *woke*?

I was still unsure, but all I knew was I felt miserable in these bikinis. I decided to buy a one-piece to have the option.

Browsing the styles, I remembered that women have one get-out-of-body-guilt-free card:

Breasts.

If God didn't want us to flaunt them, She wouldn't have put them out in front.

Sisters of the one-piece [credit: Maureen O'Connor]

So I chose a simple, black one-piece with a plunging neckline that laced up.

A good compromise between classy and trashy.

The bottom of the suit had a high-cut leg, very Bo Derek.

I get why we bailed on white girls wearing cornrows, but why did we ever abandon this style?

It's much more flattering than having the elastic cut across the mushiest part of your hip. My legs looked super long.

I could get used to this.

When the beach party rolled around, I wore my new one-piece with cutoff shorts and a gauzy white button-down. I felt good. Even sexy.

I was so emboldened, I ate breakfast.

So I get to the party and what's the first thing I see? Another guest wearing almost an identical black, lace-up, one-piece.

Was I mad?

Not in the slightest.

Women's empowerment doesn't exist without sisterhood.

World Police

Lisa

I'm exhausted from my relaxation.

Let me explain.

We begin with the fact that I'm on deadline, which means that I'm counting minutes.

Literally.

When I'm on deadline, I don't do anything social, and the only time I take off from work is to exercise, because I think it's good to keep blood flow to my brain so I can write better.

You get the idea.

I'm crazy.

Everything I do has to be justified as benefiting work, or I'm not allowed to do it. I'm not complaining. I really love writing and I've learned, in twenty-five years as a professional writer, that I have to protect my time.

But I also have to protect my sanity.

Hence, blood flow to my brain.

Which is how I came to decide the other day, after a day of writing, that it would be okay to go for a quick bike ride, then return to work that night.

In other words, I scheduled my relaxation.

It struck me as funny, considering the way I was raised. The Flying Scottolines did not schedule anything, especially not their relaxation. Both of my parents worked, and after dinner, they relaxed.

Which meant they sat in front of the television and smoked.

Then my father quit smoking, so he relaxed in front of the television and played postal chess.

Mother Mary just drove us postal.

With love.

Bottom line, when they were relaxing, they did nothing.

When I'm relaxing, I do everything.

Anyway, so my first outing on my bicycle, I'm riding from the parking lot when I see a dog jumping around frantically in a locked SUV. Part of me wants to ride by, because I'm on the relaxation schedule and I can't afford the time it would take to investigate, but then again, I love dogs and I couldn't live with myself if anything happened to the dog, so I rode to the car to see that the dog was panting and barking, worked up. And by the way, when I'd left my car, the temperature read 102 degrees inside.

You guys are smart enough to know that it can be 30° hotter in the car than outside, which is why I love you.

Unfortunately, not everyone is as smart as you.

So I went into the store and asked them to make an emergency announcement, but they refused, though that would have been best for the dog's health and the author's scheduled relaxation.

But I still couldn't turn my back on the dog, so I called 911. I waited twenty minutes, but the dog's owner arrived before the police did, so I yelled at her without the use of profanity and asked her to stop trying to kill her dog.

Then I was on my way, almost an hour late and totally cranky, which must have interfered with the blood flow to my brain because I didn't write very well when I got home.

I figured my next scheduled relaxation would be more relaxing.

But the next day, I was about to get out of my car and get on my bike when I noticed another dog being left in another car. I also noticed that the couple leaving their dog in the car hadn't gone into the store yet, so I hurried after them and told them that it wasn't safe to leave the dog in the car.

They told me they would "be just a few minutes" and "she'll be fine."

I told them that I beg to differ, it was dangerous to the dog and it was illegal.

They told me to mind my own business and it wasn't illegal.

I may have said something like, "Oh, yeah? We'll see about that!"

Again without the use of profanity.

So I called 911, though I wondered if the police would remember that I was the same lady who had called them yesterday about a different dog in a different car.

Either way, I could feel my blood rushing to my brain, and I realized that my relaxation was stressing me out.

If I were an animal-control officer, this would be my job and I could kill two birds with one stone.

But as it stands, my job requires people not to leave dogs in cars in the tristate area.

So I end this story with a plea.

To dogs.

Dogs, please do not let your completely idiotic owners, who are obviously not as smart as you, leave you in the car in the summertime.

Even with the windows "cracked."

Even for "just a few minutes."

I'm begging you, dogs.

The police have better things to do.

And I'm on deadline.

Good Morning!

Lisa

Guess who's coming over this week?

The USA.

Okay, I'm exaggerating.

But only a little.

Let me explain.

I found out that Francesca and I were scheduled to be on *Good Morning America,* which is very big news. We were booked to talk about our funny series, as well as my thrillers and novels. We were superexcited because the show has a bazillion viewers, and obviously, this would expose our books to a national audience.

But on the downside, it exposes *me* to a national audience.

And I can't be my usual slobby self.

Loyal readers know that I have recently gained weight, live in teddy-bear clothes, and let my roots go until they're incarceration-length.

Also, I have been known to pluck my chin in the car, at a stoplight.

Oh, you didn't know that?

Well, that secret has yet to be told.

Spoiler alert.

In my defense, the light is better in the car and the mirror is close enough that I can see it without my reading glasses.

Also in my defense, I saw a woman beside me doing the same thing the other day, as her husband drove.

Maybe that's why I need a husband.

To cart me around while I pluck in public.

Anyway, as soon as we got booked on *Good Morning America*, I started exercising to lose weight.

They say the camera adds ten pounds, but I disagree.

Carbohydrates add ten pounds.

I never ate a camera.

But if you bake it in a chocolate cake, stand clear.

I also scheduled an appointment to lighten my hair.

And my teeth.

I'm pretty sure Hemingway did that, too.

Okay, so far, so good.

But then the most amazing/terrifying thing happened.

Good Morning America called to say that they had changed their mind and they weren't going to have us to NYC for the show.

They said, instead . . .

Wait for it . . .

That they were going to come to the house and film us for the show *at home*.

Whaaaaatttt?

Of course this was the most amazing news ever, and it will be even better than in the studio, because it will include all the dogs, and you know how they are.

When they see a camera, they come running.

Not when we call them, however.

But what that means is not only do I have to get myself camera-ready, I have to get my entire house camera-ready.

Yikes.

First, I have to have the place cleaned.

Please note that I didn't say I would do it.

Sorry not sorry.

You can't write three books a year and do it all yourself.

I have to get cleaners to come in, but I'll clean before they

Welcome to our home, America!

Francesca and I with the great Deborah Roberts of ABC-TV's
Good Morning America

get here and after they leave, too. Because you have no idea
how much dog hair is produced in my household in one day.

And all of a sudden I'm noticing that there's dog damage
around the bottom of the door and windowsills, where their
nails dig into the wood, so I have to get busy doing something
about that.

And the rugs smell rank from you-know-what and you-
know-who, and that will have to be dealt with.

Also there are snakes in the garden.

But nobody has to know that except for us.

Well you get the idea. It's very exciting that *Good Morning
America* is going to come to the house, but it's also terrifying
that they're going to come to the house.

I mean, when was the last time I had anyone over?

And when was the last time I had *America* over?

Anyway, they're coming in two days and I barely have the time to finish writing this because I have to start gathering books, magazines, and other essential clutter, then hiding it all in my bedroom closet, where ABC-TV presumably won't go.

I have to start rearranging the furniture, so the house looks bigger.

And I have to jump on a bicycle, so that I look smaller.

I'll need hair, makeup, and a miracle.

I'll be getting the house, myself, and the tristate area ready until the very last minute, when I open the front door and say:

Good morning, America!

Blond and Blonder

Francesca

I've always hated the phrase, "dumb blonde."

I hate it even more when it applies to me.

I recently got my hair highlighted and one, little section got overbleached. It's toward the back, but it shows when I pull my hair over my shoulder, which I do often.

And I can't stop thinking about it.

I know it's dumb, I know. I feel dumb writing this now.

The modern woman faces many real challenges. We also face some made-up ones. Obsessing over your hair is the latter.

Sometimes, as women, we're prisoners of our own making. Though we can give some credit to centuries of patriarchal oppression, too. We've internalized these sexist beauty standards, and it's a battle not to let them rule our lives. Concerns about our hair, nails, and weight occupy way more mental space than they deserve.

I know better, I try to rise above, and yet . . .

Turns out I'm only "woke" enough to feel guilty for being vain and superficial.

I've been getting the same, barely there blond highlights about twice a year for the last decade. I keep the look "natural"

Highlighter's remorse

because I tell myself I'm fooling people, and because I can't afford to do it more often.

It costs a lot of money to look like you did nothing.

This last time, I had to see a new colorist. Trusting a stranger sent my preappointment anxiety into overdrive. And where do nervous women go?

Pinterest.

Because if there's one way to make yourself feel better, it's comparing yourself to others.

Soon, I had a full board of pinned images of the same three models, Gisele Bundchen, Gigi Hadid, and Rosie Huntington-Whitely, photographed with their heads at slightly different angles.

Had such a photo collection been on a real corkboard, you would alert the authorities.

Serial killer? No, just my search for killer hair.

But when I got to my appointment, I was too embarrassed to show any of the pictures to my colorist. I couldn't admit I had devoted this much time and research to my hair goals.

Oh God, I have "hair goals."

Not to mention that pointing to pictures of supermodels and demanding, "Make me look like *this,*" feels far-fetched.

There's only bleach in that bottle, not a genie.

So instead I gestured vaguely, said words like "warm" and "summery," and pretended to be chill.

When we were all done, the reflection in the mirror was brighter and lighter than I had expected, but she did a beautiful job. I looked like a bombshell.

Yet, immediately I zeroed in on that too-bright patch.

Because that's another thing women are great at: focusing on the flaw.

Passing every shop window on the way home, and catching myself in every mirror in my apartment, my eyes darted to that bleach splotch. And when I couldn't see it, I could feel it, mocking me with its trashy fakeness.

While the rest of my head was pulling off a plausible I-just-got-back-from-vacation blond, this lemon-yellow stripe was calling my bluff.

But another part of my brain, the part with a college degree and the right to vote, hated that this bothered me. I decided I would just get over it. It would be good for me, at best, a growing experience.

At worst, a growing-out experience.

I made it three days.

Then I went back to the salon, full of apologies and re-hearsed explanations, and asked if she could tone that one section down.

"Oh sure. I can fix it no problem."

Twenty minutes later, the offending swath had been cor-rected and blended perfectly into the rest.

The fog of beauty angst lifted. I was returned to myself again.

Maybe the lesson is that true empowerment is asking for what you want without fear of judgment. Maybe empower-ment is being less self-critical, even of our more superficial desires. Maybe empowerment is the perfect shade of blond.

Nah, it's really only hair.

And someday I'll grow out of caring so much.

Potted

Lisa

Many things are harder than they look.

The best example of this is marriage.

The second best is houseplants.

As we all know, I'm divorced twice.

But we may not know that I cannot grow a houseplant to save my life.

Guess which thing I regret.

Heh heh.

Our houseplant drama begins last summer, after I had started a garden in front of the house, which I'm completely in love with. It has all sorts of pretty perennials like black-eyed Susan, lavender, coneflower, and a whole bunch of other flowers that I secretly take credit for growing.

Never mind the fact that it's the perfect location, on a hill protected from wind, nurtured by full-day sun, with excellent soil, since this used to be a dairy farm.

Still, I take credit.

I mean, why not?

I bought the plants, which should count for something.

And I pay somebody to weed, which should also count for something.

Okay, all I do with this garden is look at it, smell the roses, and avoid the snakes.

No, they haven't returned yet. I'm holding my breath. Maybe on Halloween?

In any event, because the garden worked out so well and made me so happy, I thought it would be nice to start growing plants inside. I'm probably the only person on earth who never bothered with houseplants, mainly because I have so many damn pets that require full-time attention, especially Ruby. She's the crazy corgi who unfortunately got DM, paralysis of her hind, which means that she has to be in a wheelie cart and lately, has to be diapered three times a day.

Great.

You haven't lived until you've had an incontinent corgi.

I know I'm not alone in this, because the diaper aisle at the pet store is huge and even has diaper liners, which are like big sanitary napkins that you can stick on your own panties and put on your dog, if you happen to run out of doggie diapers and don't feel like driving to the pet store.

Not that that has ever happened.

But Ruby looks pretty good in a pair of size 6 Hanes, bikini-cut.

So you see why I was in no rush to start with the houseplants, but I thought it would be nice, and around the same I time was thinking this, I found out that *Good Morning America* was coming to the house, which meant that I ordered a bunch of indoor flowers, so I could pretend I'm the kind of woman who lives in a house with fresh-cut flowers.

Instead of the kind of woman who dresses up an incontinent corgi in her own underwear.

And while I was on the phone with the florist, they said they were having a sale on indoor hydrangea, which were a very pretty blue, and since I have pink hydrangea outside, I thought it would be nice to have blue hydrangea inside, so I ordered three potted hydrangeas.

Beautiful while they lasted

I thought, how hard could it be to grow them inside?

I mean, buy a potted plant and water it.

Isn't it even an expression, "sitting there like a potted plant?"

It should be dumb and easy.

So the indoor hydrangea looked gorgeous for the *Good Morning America* shoot, but after that, it was Goodbye Hydrangea.

The flowers started to die, so I watered them more. Then I went online, and it said not to water them too much.

So then I didn't water them at all for about four days, but they just kept dying.

They're supposed to be fine in indirect light, but I moved them into the sun, and they still kept dying, then moved them into a shady part of the house, and they were completely dead.

Then I went back online and it said that indoor hydrangea can be shocked back to life with very very hot water, and I did that.

And you know what?

It actually worked.

The plants perked up and started to grow new leaves.

My heart soared.

Until two days later, when all of the leaves started to get white spots on them, that looked suspiciously moldy. So I went back online and discovered that they actually were mold, and one of the remedies suggested spraying the plants with a solution of one quarter milk and three-quarters water.

Which I did.

Now the whole house smells like curdling milk, the plants

remain spotted and molding, and the ones that aren't moldy are dying.

God knows why.

It looked easy, but it wasn't.

Next time, I'm ordering fresh-cut flowers.

Because that's the kind of woman I am.

Happy Birthday

Lisa

By the time you read this, I will be a year older.

But no wiser.

Because I almost got killed this morning doing a dumb thing.

Or maybe the best thing I ever did.

You be the judge.

We began on a quiet Saturday morning, and I was going to meet my best friend Franca so we could ride our bikes on the trail.

Yes, it's that time of year again, when Franca and I go bicycle-riding and try to remain upright.

I was driving to meet her, and there was only light traffic because it was early in the morning on a summer weekend, but as I turned onto this main, four-lane road near my house, I happened to notice a flock of mother and baby geese about to step off the curb on the other side of the street and cross the road.

So right away, you know where this is going.

We're in world-police territory.

And I could tell what was going to happen. There was a

car stopped at a red light at this major intersection, and the mommy goose had just stepped off the curb to make her way across four lanes of inevitable death.

I couldn't watch, but I couldn't ignore it, and I certainly couldn't do nothing.

So I pulled the car over, parked in the turn lane, and put on my blinker, then jumped out and started yelling, "Stop!"

I think I was yelling to the cars, like, "stop, don't kill me!" or "stop, don't kill the baby geese!" or maybe even "stop me from doing something stupid like this, because I'm older and should know better!"

But the general idea was STOP.

I ran across the two lanes toward the geese but there were two cars coming toward me. I told myself not to worry, that I was plainly visible and I was waving my arms like a mad-woman and any idiot could see what the problem was. One of the cars slowed to a stop, evidencing respect for human and avian life, but the other one not only didn't stop, but ac-tually drove around me without even slowing down.

I cursed, at decibel level.

The other car honked.

So did the geese.

Unfortunately they also scattered in about twenty-five different directions, all over the road.

I tried to shoo them back to the curb and a few of them went, but they freaked as more and more cars started arriv-ing on the scene, most of them stopping but many not even breaking stride at the sight of a middle-aged woman on the eve of her birthday, frantically trying to convince random geese to obey her when her own dogs will not.

Luckily, the geese started to get the idea, fleeing away from me, the yelling drivers, and racing cars, and they waddled back to the grass where they had been, then I ran back across the street to my car. But I was worried that they were going to try to cross again and I knew I needed help.

My law-enforcement specialty is dogs-in-hot-cars, not geese-trying-to-commit-suicide.

So I called my good friends at 911.

Don't think I take this lightly because I know emergencies are a serious thing, but I thought this qualified, and I am newly deputized to protect all animal life.

Still I half expected the dispatcher to answer, "Lisa, again?"

Or, "Don't you ever mind your own business?"

But they didn't, and they sent out a police car, with the happy ending that the geese were saved and I was able to complete my bike ride.

I didn't even fall down.

Or get run over.

It might've been the best birthday ever.

And I'm taking cake to the cops.

Pushed Around

Lisa

You know what a cutlet is?

Men think it's something you eat for dinner.

But women know better.

For those of you without estrogen, a cutlet is a piece of fake-cotton padding in a bra.

And all of a sudden, cutlets are everywhere, aren't they?

I say this because I went online shopping for bathing suits, which taught me many new things about the world of fashion.

Before I begin, let me explain why I was shopping online for bathing suits instead of going to a store.

Exactly.

That requires no explanation.

There is nothing that will kill your soul faster than going into an actual fitting room and trying on bathing suits in the horrible fluorescent lighting, hoping that the store surveillance system does not include some unlucky schmo whose job it is to watch you squeeze your cellulite into what is allegedly a medium.

Enough said.

Plus I don't care what the bathing suit looks like. I know

my size, the aforementioned medium, and all I want is a simple two-piece bathing suit so I can doggie-paddle around in my pool. And yes, I wear a two-piece because it's fun to run around half-naked, especially if your only audience is four Cavalier King Charles spaniels and a handicapped corgi.

I doggie-paddle with doggies.

Anyway, my old bathing suit was looking crappy, so I decided to get a new bathing suit and went online shopping. I clicked around, found some decent two-piece suits, added them to my online shopping cart, then went to check out. But when I double-checked the order, I found that I had ordered bathing-suit tops, but no bottoms.

What?

I went back to the webpage, where I realized that nowadays, bathing-suit tops are sold without bottoms.

Why?

I had just assumed that a bathing suit included a top and a bottom.

Because I'm normal.

Who buys a top without a bottom?

My first thought was, people are having way too much fun in summer.

Then I realized that it was probably because people wanted to get different sizes for different body parts, and I guess that's progress, but then the website didn't even suggest which bottom went with which top. In fact, under each bathing-suit top, there was the standard shopping suggestion, IF YOU LIKE THIS, YOU MIGHT ALSO LIKE, but the suggestions were for cover-ups, not for the correct bottom to the top.

Which left me completely confused.

Normally I'm a sucker for IF YOU LIKE THIS, YOU MIGHT ALSO LIKE, not to mention PEOPLE WHO LIKE THIS ALSO BOUGHT, but perhaps I'm putting too much faith in PEOPLE.

Anyway, to make a long story short, it turned out there was a whole separate section on the website for bathing-suit bottoms, and I spent the next hour trying to find a bottom for the top, whether it matched or not, which is another new thing.

In the olden days, the top of the bathing suit matched the bottom.

But no longer.

All this progress.

Now we get to design our own bathing suits.

What happened to keep it simple, stupid?

And oddly, none of the bottoms that remotely matched was in stock—though all of the tops were, which I cannot begin to understand or explain.

Who's buying more bottoms than tops?

Whatever the reason, it made shopping for bottoms a pain in the bottom.

(I kept that joke clean for you.)

And it also proved that shopping for bathing suits online could be just as soul-killing as shopping in an actual store.

A bricks-and-mortar store.

Because evidently, bricks-and-mortar goes together more certainly than top-and-bottom.

To stay on point, when the bathing suits arrived, each of them had cutlets in the tops, which I removed instantly, on principle.

If I wanted a push-up bra, I would've ordered one.

I mean, what's the point?

Do I have to look busty for my dogs?

(By the way, Busty is a great word *and* a great dog name, which never happens.)

Or are we supposed to hide our nipples?

World, we have nipples.

Deal with it.

I thought it was ironic that tops came with cutlets but not with bottoms.

Maybe the idea was that you wear the cutlets as a bottom?

Tape two together, front and back.

Like a fig leaf made of Lycra.

Anyway, I'm not a cutlet fan.

Cutlets are not just for dinner anymore.

Can't a woman catch a break?

Isn't there any time we don't have to worry about what we look like?

I say the time is now.

Every woman deserves to relax, especially in July, floating around half-naked in front of dogs or people.

That's the very definition of summer.

Ladies, throw away your cutlets.

Don't let anybody push you around.

Or up.

Beach Bums

Francesca

People-watching on the beach is a time-honored tradition. Looking at the ocean is our communal alibi, sunglasses are the universal disguise, but we all know what we're up to. But despite the smorgasbord of humanity that parades past, there are certain beach bums who show up in one form or another every time. See if you've ever run into one of these characters, or if you happen to be reading this on the beach, let's play a little game of I Spy . . .

The DJ. This is the person who thinks they're doing you a favor by pumping their crappy music through crappier plastic speakers. Because why would you want to enjoy the sounds of the waves or children laughing when you can listen to Top 40 music from two seasons ago remixed to the speed of a jump-rope workout? Do not attempt to engage the DJ by politely requesting they turn it down—these people are overgrown teenagers, any attempt to educate them will only inspire defiance. The only recourse is to give them a withering gaze over your sunglasses as you gather your things to find a new towel spot.

The Wipeout Artist. This person is an ER visit waiting to happen. A frat bro doing backflips into shallow water. A teenage girl practicing wobbly round-offs on packed sand. A kid venturing into rough surf with a boogie board twice his size. Whatever they're doing, it looks like a bad idea. You watch with a mixture of motherly concern and schadenfreude.

The Smoker. Smokers, I get it. We've precluded you from smoking in all your favorite places, restaurants, bars, airports. I'll anticipate your argument: nobody owns the beach! Who are we, holier-than-thou nonsmokers to say you can't enjoy a few puffs as we all pee in the ocean? You have a point. But the charm of a day at the beach is the natural beauty and the fresh sea air. And it's a bummer when you see a little kid making a sandcastle with a Marlboro chimney.

The Mammarelle. This term might be exclusive to Italian-American dialect, but you know who I mean: the little old lady who stands at the edge of the surf. She hasn't updated her swimwear since the days when they called it a "bathing costume," but she doesn't care; time has washed away all fashion and body insecurities, thank God. Either she can't swim, or she doesn't swim, but she surely has no fear—she stands, still and unflinching, as huge waves crash or a body-boarder swerves around her or a football whizzes by her head. Her activities are limited to gently crouching and splashing water on her thighs, disapproving of children, and staring out at the horizon with the wisdom of the ages. She is as salty as the sea itself. I want to be her.

The Missing Link. This guy has a back so hairy, it looks like he's wearing a fur cape. To be completely honest, I love this guy. I never make fun of him. Human enjoyment of the beach is so pure, it feels primal. We're all animals, this guy especially, and we should all feel free to enjoy the breeze on our skin and the sun on our shoulders. He's a symbol of body acceptance we could all stand to emulate.

Disclosure: I once dated a guy in college who had the furriest back and shoulders, and I *shaved the back of his neck for him* so that, in his words, "there would be a break" between his head hair and his back hair. Readers, if you have a son or brother who is single, think of this and what a nice girlfriend I can be.

The Bad Parent. If you sit at the beach long enough, you're gonna see somebody smack their kid. Then you have to decide whether saying something will make it better or worse. Here's the thing, kids at the beach are going to kick sand, and steal toys, and not come in from the surf when you tell them to, they're kids! My theory is that parents feel more on display at the beach, so they overreact to their children's misbehavior. The irony is, the fear of judgment that makes them react harshly is exactly what incurs that judgment from others. My request to the bad parent is this: if I promise to give you the benefit of the doubt this one time, will you please find a better way to discipline your kid?

The Lovers. Honestly, I'm more grossed out by these people than the hairy guy. Look, you already get to be nearly naked and lying down next to each other. You even get to lube each other up with suntan oil. I will allow a few kisses on top of all that. But if you need MORE erotic interaction than what I just listed, please, for the sake of the children, go home.

The Space Invaders. Um, hi, we're right here, in case you didn't notice. I think you did notice, because you just kicked your sandy flip-flops off onto my blanket. Your cooler just nudged my head. Your bag of chips just tipped over onto my magazines. You know I am here. More importantly, you know I was here first. So please, just acknowledge me and my personal space so we can work this out. On a crowded beach, a simple, "is this okay?" turneth away wrath.

The Loud Talker. A beach is not a library, it's the great outdoors, knock yourself out! The beach is a symphony of sound: the crashing waves, the propeller airplanes, the children squealing in the surf, their mothers calling to them. But there are some people whose voices cut through the din like a squawking seagull. You try to refocus on the page of your book— maybe even this book!—but you can't ignore them. You're transformed into an unwilling eavesdropper, listening to a boring story about their mother-in-law or the football game or lunch plans or Susan's divorce. (Susan, I'm sorry, but it sounds like you're better off.) I don't know if it's the volume of their voice or the timbre or the direction of the wind. The truth is, it isn't their fault, but I blame them for it anyway.

The Angel Child. Maybe it's just me and my ovaries going "knock knock, anybody home?" but I always get fixated on one magical child at the beach. Last time it was a family with three kids under age six who squeezed in next to me and my friend. I confess, when I first saw them setting out their things so close to us, I worried this was too many kids-per-square-foot of sand, but these kids were a dream. The older brother and sister played nicely with one another, but the youngest was the sweetest of all. She sat under the umbrella with her dad and watched her siblings, squeezing the sand in tiny fist-fuls, her hair in little beaded braids, her head as perfect and round as a marigold. Later, we gathered our things to go home, I stopped to tell their mother how sweet her kids were and that "anyone should be so lucky" to sit next to her family at the beach.

That's the wonderful thing about the beach, it's small enough to fit everyone, no matter their wacky habits and body-hairstyles, without bothering anyone too much. Any petty irritation is outweighed by our common goal—to relax and let the sun, sand, and water ease summertime into our bones.

Even better than watching beach bums is becoming one yourself.

Work Zoned

Lisa

Francesca and I just returned from book tour, driving to bookstores in Maryland, Delaware, Pennsylvania, Connecticut, and Cape Cod. It was wonderful to meet our readers, and the only downside of the tour was the fault of the Pennsylvania Turnpike Commission.

Let me explain.

I'm not the bravest driver in the world, especially when I'm crossing the Bay Bridge in Maryland. In fact, Francesca drove us over the bridge while I was in the passenger seat, driving myself over the deep end.

I would like to meet the person who designed the Bay Bridge, which zooms straight up into the clouds, veers left at a seagull, reaches heaven, then plunges back down again, barely skimming the top of the briny deep.

It's not a bridge, it's a roller coaster.

I had been dreading the Bay Bridge since before the tour started, when I looked at Google Maps, determined that we had to cross the bridge, then noticed an article reporting the bridge was so terrifying that there's a service whereby people will drive your car over the bridge for you.

While you pee yourself in the backseat.

The cost for this service is $25, but I would've paid $250, though unfortunately, the service has to be booked a few months in advance because sanity still exists.

I wish I could meet the people who booked the service. I feel sure that my future ex-husband would be among them.

So Francesca got us over the bridge, but I took the wheel when we crossed into Pennsylvania, where I got mad at my own Commonwealth. Because when I wasn't looking, the Turnpike Commission raised the speed limit to 70. Of course, if the speed limit is 70, everyone's going 75 and even 80, with the result that your favorite author (me), was doing 55 in the slow lane.

Because I still remember 55 Stay Alive.

In fact, I could find statistics that prove that there are fewer accidents at a speed limit of 55, but I can't look it up right now as I am still shaking from driving on the Pennsylvania Turnpike.

Anyway, you don't need statistics when you have common sense, and it makes sense that if you drive slower, you're less likely to have an accident. Or if you have an accident, it's less likely to be one that turns you into middle-aged road pizza.

In any event, you can imagine how the trip through Pennsylvania went, as I drove in the slow lane doing a completely sensible 55, but was nevertheless honked, tailgated, and given the finger 55 times, which I'm pretty sure was a coincidence.

Needless to say, my beloved daughter watched cars passing us with increasing horror. "Mom," Francesca said, "you have to speed up."

"No, I refuse."

"But this isn't a safe speed."

"Incorrect. I'm the only one going a safe speed. Every other single person on the highway is going an unsafe speed."

Mutual unhappiness ensued.

The only time I felt relaxed was when when we drove through a work zone, where the speed limit lowered to 40 and everyone else drove at snail's pace, too.

World Order, restored.

I love the work zone. I would live in the work zone if I could. Orange really is the new black.

Everyone else complains about highway construction.

I pray for it.

Otherwise, I felt most scared by big trucks, and when I saw them behind me, I would put on my hazard lights to let them know that I was a nervous author driving at a speed limit that doesn't exist anymore.

Some of them passed me, but others rode my bumper, flashed their lights, and gunned their engines, and I can't tell you that I thought nice things about them. That is, until a lovely woman at one of our signings said that she loved our books and also that she was a trucker.

She bought a book, and I liked truckers all over again.

I'm easy that way.

But by the end of the trip, which also took us over the Falls River Bridge in Massachusetts, as well as the Bourne and the Sagamore Bridges in Cape Cod, I hated driving altogether. Even when Francesca was doing the driving, which she was, in all of the above.

So this is my message to my amazing daughter, who showed skill and courage behind the wheel:

We survived thanks to Francesca!

Thank you.

And this is my message to the Pennsylvania Turnpike Commission, who made me feel unsafe on the roads of my very own state:

Okay, forget it, I'll keep it clean.

The American Dream

Lisa

You may remember that I wrote previously about wanting to add a little room onto my kitchen so that I could look at a blooming garden instead of a stainless steel wall.

I went back and forth about whether I was entitled to spend money that was supposed to be for my retirement on a home renovation that I might not even live to see, since I am half-dead already, at sixty-one.

Well, thanks to your wonderful encouraging emails and also my innate selfishness and inability to delay gratification, I am building the garden room, and we just broke ground.

And rapidly thereafter, we ran into a wall.

Literally.

They dug a big hole for the concrete pad and found an underground wall, which of course led to heavy orange equipment and costly change orders, but I'm not complaining.

I'm getting my garden room and praying I live long enough to enjoy it.

My current dilemma is typical of the kind of thing that construction presents, which is that as soon as you fix one thing, you need to fix another.

As in I thought it would be nice to have a little fenced-in area around the garden, so the dogs could enjoy the garden, too, and hang out with me when I weed.

Wait, that's a lie.

I don't weed anymore.

I used to weed, in fact I was becoming vaguely compulsive about weeding, but then I realize I had to quit cold turkey, mainly because it was making me crazy, a job that is never ever done like making your bed, another job I ignore.

Plus I realized that summer is only three months long and even weeds can't grow that much in three months, so what I'm doing now is waiting the weeds out. They can take up residence through August, because that's all that's left, but they're going to be dead by September.

Joke's on them.

So there you have it.

Weeds grow in my garden.

Guess what?

The world didn't end.

In fact, I'm going to call my garden room my weed-and-garden room, and it will still be great to have, even if I don't get to retire until 2085.

To stay on point, I thought it would be fun to have the dogs run around the garden, but there is no fence there, and they can run onto the driveway or even the street. So I'm going to put up a fence, and what I've secretly always wanted is a white picket fence.

Am I a walking cliché, or what?

I grew up hearing all about the white picket fence, and knowing that it meant you were supposed to be married, have

2.3 children, a dog, and a cat. Then later, the white picket fence became a dumb thing to want, signifying oppression of all sorts, or bourgeois taste in general.

To this, I plead guilty.

Because I want a white picket fence. Even though I'm divorced twice, live alone, have one cat who won't speak to me, and five dogs—one of which is in a wheelchair and a diaper and still manages to poop on the floor.

That's the kind of talent that runs in the Scottoline blood.

I called up a fence guy and told him I wanted a white picket fence. He told me the prices were very reasonable, except they doubled when we got to the white part. "What's the deal?" I asked him.

"It's really expensive to paint a white picket fence, and it's a lot of trouble and expense to maintain. You should just get the cedar. That's what everybody does."

"But whoever heard of a cedar picket fence? It's not the same thing."

"You're right, it's not. It's half as much money."

"But a white picket fence is the American dream. The fences are supposed to be white picket, not cedar picket. These are clichés for reason. I know, I'm a writer."

The fence guy didn't laugh. "I still think you should get the cedar. Everybody else does."

I gave up, looking at the costs. "Okay," I said.

I gave up on the white picket fence.

Like everybody else in America.

But you know what happened next, because you get who I am as a person, as a woman, and as a spendthrift in general.

The more I thought about it, the more I wanted a white

picket fence. I pictured it with white climbing roses and a trellis, which would add to its cost, and as we all know, the goal is for me to spend every last penny of my retirement fund.

The climbing roses would be dripping petals over a lovely trellis, with blooms the exact hue of the fence itself, which would be white.

A soft white, like cream.

My American Cream.

Friends, I'm writing that check, right now.

The View from the Ferry

Francesca

That weekend in August, it felt like the city had a fever about to break.

The moment you stepped outside, the heat made you weak, and the humidity made you woozy. It made you mad it was so hot, and that anger gave you the little energy you needed to get wherever you had to go.

I knew I was in for it when it felt this way at eight in the morning. My friend and I had made plans to spend the day at Rockaway Beach, since being outdoors and not near a body of water seemed unthinkable. My friend was biking to the beach from her apartment in Brooklyn, while I planned to take the 9:30 A.M. ferry for the first time.

This is why New York City residents flee in August. In the dead of summer, the city becomes a hot box of sun-reflecting asphalt and concrete. Tall buildings block the breeze, and the humidity has nowhere to go but hang heavy. The smells of the city, never the most appealing bouquet, are magnified, with each scent conjuring its solid form as clearly as if you'd stepped in it.

The streets were relatively deserted. My missing neighbors

were either hiding in the air-conditioning or, I imagined, de-
camped to their beach rentals or European holidays. Work
demands had conspired against me this summer, so I wasn't
getting any vacation, and today's beach day-trip was my consolation prize. As I passed each empty block, drops of self-
pity formed like beads of sweat.

I had to take the subway to South Seaport. Underground,
it felt like a convection oven. Once inside the subway car,
weak air-conditioning whirring provided some relief, and as
the car was almost empty, I spread out my limbs like a star-
fish and tried to think cool thoughts.

As the 1 train rattled farther downtown, more people got
on. Two Muslim girls wearing pastel hijabs got on and started
giggling about something on their phone. At the next stop, a
couple who looked of Indian descent boarded with a young
child in a stroller. The baby perked me up a little. He had
big brown eyes with eyelashes long enough to cast shade, and
he casually hung one leg out of the stroller to catch some air.

I feel ya, kid.

The mother and I shared a smile.

It's typical to see New Yorkers of different races, religions,
and ethnicities, speaking different languages, so I assumed
they were residents. But when a family of very tall Germans
boarded sporting backpacks, classic tourist giveaway, I remembered that I was on a train headed toward several major
tourist destinations: the 9/11 Museum and the ferry dock to
visit Ellis Island and the Statue of Liberty.

I've lived here for eight years and I haven't visited either
spot.

My mom and I are always talking about visiting Ellis Island, but we haven't gotten around to it. I made a mental note for her next visit.

My guess was confirmed once we emerged above ground at South Seaport to more of a crowd than I thought, and my fellow subway riders joined the people surrounding the tour guides who camp out at this station. I always want tourists to have a fun time, so I felt sorry for the infernal weather and wondered if they regretted coming this time of year. But the mood of the crowd was happy and excited. I weaved around people cracking open brochures and guidebooks and walked the opposite direction in the blazing sun to the pier for the Rockaway Beach ferry.

I was among the first in line to board, and I snagged a seat on the upper deck, where I hoped the most wind would hit once we got moving. I had given up worrying about my frizzed hair or sweaty upper lip, as everyone looked equally wilted and shiny. The communal grossness bred solidarity.

And you could feel the collective mood lift once we lurched off the dock and got onto the water. The breeze was refreshing, and people who had previously been sour and silent perked up into chatter and taking photos. A woman took a seat next to me, looking rather elegant in a green sarong. Feeling the friendly mood, I complimented her.

We got to talking, an easy conversation about the weather, New York City real estate, books, and eventually what we did for a living. I told her I was a writer, and she said she wanted to write a book.

She was a human-rights lawyer at the UN representing the needs of refugee children. She was a refugee herself; she had

The city I'm lucky to call home

spent much of her early childhood in a refugee camp fleeing the Bosnian War, before immigrating to the United States with her parents. She said she also wanted to write a children's book about a refugee child, so that some of the children she works with wouldn't feel so alone, and so that they would know their story could have a happy ending like hers did.

A happy ending in America.

And did I think that was a good idea for a book?

I was awestruck. I told her I thought it sounded like a wonderful book, and she should absolutely write it.

We pulled past Governor's Island, and the Statue of Liberty came into view.

The sight gave me a chill.

That morning, I was desperate to get out of the hot, sticky, smelly city that New Yorkers flee in August.

And now I was looking at the symbol of hope, opportunity, and acceptance for so many.

I glanced back to the beautiful, shining, city I was lucky to call home.

Everything looked so different from the ferry.

For the Win

Lisa

I don't know where to begin.

But here we go.

You may recall that Francesca and I were asked to make an appearance on Ladies' Night at the Philadelphia Phillies, attend a fun party with Phillies fans before the game, and I was invited to throw out a ceremonial first pitch.

So behind the scenes, as soon as I got this news, I felt two things at once.

Excitement and panic.

The excitement is easy to describe. I've lived in Philadelphia all of my life, and I love the Phillies. I grew up with the Phillies, and the game was always on in our house and every Sunday when we would visit my Uncle Rocky, Uncle Mikey, and Uncle Dominic.

The Flying Scottolines have a long history of watching other people do strenuous things.

My aunts watched, too, but they would have the TV on in the kitchen, while they were making gravy.

Sunday was not a Ladies' Afternoon.

By the way, as much as we loved the Phillies, The Flying

A dream come true!

Scottolines never went to the games because that would have required leaving the couch.

Also, we would eat Sunday dinner during the game, and ravioli doesn't travel easy.

In my family, the only thing that trumps the Phillies is carbohydrates.

So to stay on point, the panic of being asked to throw out the first pitch is that I don't know how to pitch.

I Googled "how to pitch" online and came up with vid-

AW!

eos that talked about "pitching mechanics," "thumbs down," "full windup," "pronate your throwing hand," and you get the idea, a "nightmare."

I told my friends that I was going to be throwing out the

first pitch, and they sent me videos of people younger and more male than I am throwing terrible pitches, but that only made me worry more. I immediately went into hyperdrive, buying a mitt and a ball, and vowing to practice every day, which did not happen.

Mainly because I have a job and it does not involve learning to pitch.

And also I went on book tour where I pitched my book, which is not the same thing.

Luckily, I'm working on a book about a baseball player, and I was researching it with the Great Valley High School baseball team, and Coach Matthew Schultz, and the guys were kind enough to give me a pitching lesson. Plus, my best friend and assistant, Laura, came over with her teenage sons, Shane and Liam, who are not only great young men but great baseball players, and they both gave me pitching lessons.

Bottom line, I had a pitching staff of thirty.

For one woman, and one pitch.

Why?

Because on Ladies' Night, there was one thing I wanted *not* to do, at all costs:

I didn't want to Throw Like A Girl.

I wanted to overcome all clichés.

I didn't want to embarrass all womankind.

I wanted to represent those of us with ovaries.

In short, I wanted to reach the plate.

And I wanted the ball to go straight.

No pressure.

Anyway, to make a long story short, Ladies' Night was amazing, starting with Francesca and me getting real Phillies jerseys with our names on the back, which were long enough to cover my butt.

Yay!

Then we went to our pregame event, partied with a huge crew of Phillies fans, and met the great radio host Jim Jackson, and all the time we were kept on schedule by the incredibly adorable and efficient Catherine and Vanessa, who made sure that I got to the field on time for the first pitch.

The Phillies Organization is well organized.

Heading out for my first Major League appearance

A home run of a daughter!

They should run the country.

And then there I was, on a gorgeous summer night, standing in front of the pitcher's mound before God-knows-how-many Phillies fans at Citizens Bank Park. The stadium is way bigger than it looks on TV, especially if you're standing all alone, at its center.

I felt like an ant in the middle of an empty spaghetti bowl.

A girl ant.

Then the Philly Phanatic, whom I adore, took home plate to be my catcher.

And it was my moment of truth.

Deep breath.

I tried to remember everything that my pitching staff had taught me.

And I threw the ball, which amazingly, went all the way to the Phanatic's oversized glove and didn't even bounce! And not only that, it went straight and not to either side like 50 Cent, Michael Jordan, or even Gary Dell'Abate from the *Howard Stern Show!*

Yay!

Baba-booey!

Amazing!

Thanks so much to my coaches, and most of all, to the Philadelphia Phillies, who even won that night!

So in the end, I didn't Throw Like a Girl at all.

I Threw Like a *Woman*.

Back to School

Lisa

Okay, summer is over and we're collectively bummed.

The consolation prize is school supplies.

No, I'm not twelve years old.

But I still love school supplies.

If I could buy a protractor, I might be the happiest person on earth.

Or even a pencil case, which I can't justify since I don't even use pencils.

Or how about a ruler, an old-school wooden one, but I don't measure even my waist anymore.

But still, maybe I could buy a pencil case and put things in it, like a laptop.

Nothing makes me happier than a fresh pack of printer paper, even though I can't remember the last time I printed anything.

And I need new printer ink, so I can put it into my printer and let it dry up.

But truly, I do love new legal pads, canary yellow and ready for fresh litigation.

Please tell me I'm not the only alleged adult who feels this way.

Who finds her internal clock geared to the school year, even though she's not a student anymore, and even though the student she raised has grown up and moved to New York City.

It's just that at this time of year, I usually find an excuse to get myself into Staples, where I lose three hours browsing three-ring notebooks.

I look at every type of Post-it available and choose carefully which colors will change my life, or failing that, organize me better.

I'm thinking that the lure of school supplies, as you get older, has more to do with a wish for organization and productivity.

In other words, the mental riff is something like, the air is turning colder, and I'm getting back to business.

No more fooling around.

Summer is for losers, and fall is for winners.

Now I'm going to make myself into a winner, and get things done!

I'm going to write things down and do all the Things on my Things To Do List.

And for that I need, obviously, pink index cards, double-sided tape, binders in different colors, and special dividers with tabs you can see through and perforated white inserts that are too small to fit your handwriting.

Also multicolored file folders for bills I never file.

And a desk organizer for paper clips I use to pick my teeth.

A metal easel with a giant pad for plotting novels, though I have never outlined a single one.

My surprise endings come as a surprise to me.

And of course, pens.

I don't think it's because I'm a writer, I think it's because I'm a human being in September, but the fact is, I have a primal urge to go out and acquire pens.

I'll spend an hour in the pen aisle in a quest for the perfect pen, searching through an array of fine-point, medium-point, and big-ass-point pens.

Also called bold point.

Guess which one I picked.

I identify.

And not just because of the aforementioned ass, but because I'm not a fine-point kind of girl. I'm not subtle or delicate.

Nor am I middle-of-the-road, neither here nor there, so medium doesn't appeal to me.

I like the biggest point possible, to make the biggest point possible, and also, frankly, so I can read it.

Because I'm not twelve years old.

So of course what always happens is that I buy a bag of pens, bring them home, and think they are perfect, so perfect that I practically hoard them, and then, God knows how, I can't find them anymore.

Every September I buy too many pens and yet somehow, I can never find a pen in my house.

The other day, I had to write a check and I went to three different rooms looking for a pen, and ultimately I found one in my purse.

On the pen it read, Marriott Hotels.

Go figure.

And have a great school year.

Girl Vitamin

Francesca

Why do men expect women to cure them?

Is it the mom thing? It's the mom thing, isn't it?

But why do we fall for it?

I'm as guilty of it as anyone. I never date jerks. I date sensitive guys, men in touch with their needs and their feelings.

They just aren't in touch with mine.

But I swear I'm not ferreting these men out, they aren't needles in haystacks.

They're the hay.

They're everywhere! Every guy in black jeans thinks he's Johnny Cash looking for his June to set him straight.

The fantasy is twofold: that the man is the star, the lovably flawed hero of the story, and the woman is a supporting player, there to clean up his mess and set him on his destiny.

It's like the women's movement got just far enough to convince men they no longer need to take care of us and stopped dead.

Sure, it's progress that wives no longer need to ask for allowances and call their husbands "Daddy."

But we didn't work that hard to become Mommy and take care of our partners in perpetual boyhood.

That isn't empowerment; it's women catering to the male ego from a different angle.

Why is it so hard to find an equal partner?

Maybe because we women convince ourselves this rescue fantasy is romantic.

We're conditioned to find male helplessness endearing. Like it's a fun, prebaby challenge to our nurturing sides, or a roundabout way to ensure a man's loyalty and devotion via total dependence.

We've been sold a fairy tale of a damaged man who needs us desperately, from Mr. Rochester to Jerry Maguire.

We've repeated, *I've repeated*, the same pattern of overfunctioning in relationships, then being shocked when the man doesn't step up.

I'm tired of the "you make me a better man" line.

If a girl makes a guy feel like a better man, it's probably because she washed the dishes he left in the sink.

Listen, I'm not telling men they have to be perfect. We are all a work in progress.

But women aren't the construction workers and men the glorious monument. The building up and support has to go both ways.

When I'm not exhausted by man-baby behavior, I'm actually a very nurturing person. I enjoy doting on my partner, and I try to be generous in all my relationships. I only want to find a man who won't take advantage of it.

Somehow, even when I explicitly try to avoid this dynamic, it sucks me back in.

I started seeing a guy who was open about how he had often dated girls who needed him to fix them. And I thought, *yes!* Finally, a man who *gets it*.

After all, it goes both ways. Just as women suffer from the Mr. Rochester trope, the damsel-in-distress narrative unfairly burdens men.

I was ready to jump into a post-fairy-tale romance.

But then he couldn't stop talking about those exes. He compared me to them constantly:

"You're so different from . . ."

". . . used to always do that. But you're nothing like her."

The only compliment he gave me that wasn't relative to another woman was, "You're exactly what I need."

It raised concerns, but I wrote them off. I admit, I was flattered. And I told myself that this was the sort of self-reflection in a man that I'd been looking for. That he happened to think aloud was unfortunate, but not a deal-breaker.

Nobody's perfect.

I felt like we were stuck in our heads, well, his head, so for our third date, I suggested dinner and dancing to loosen up.

We didn't make it that far. Before they brought the check, he asked, "Should we talk about how this is going or just go dancing?"

Post-fairy-tale indeed.

I told him it sounded like a rhetorical question, but he insisted I go first. I brought up the ex-talk.

"I feel like you're viewing me in opposition to these other girls, like I'm the antidote. But I'm a person, too. I'm not a girl-vitamin."

He burst into laughter. He told me I was exactly right, that "girl vitamin" was "perfect" and "so apt."

He wagged a finger at me. "That's why you're a writer."

Thanks?

He explained that he thought I would be good for him, that I'd break his bad habits with women, but "I guess I don't feel that spark with you."

No thanks.

So I have a message for all the men out there:

Women don't exist to complete or inspire or cure you.

Women are not vitamins.

Women are not muses.

Women are not anchors.

Women are not crutches.

Women are not your mom.

Loving us may make you happier, healthier, more motivated, or more responsible, but that's not our sole reason for being.

Take your vitamins.

Then give us a call.

Which Spices Would You Take to a Kitchen Island?

Lisa

There's nothing like home improvement to improve your life.

At least, not in theory.

I say this because I'm adding a garden room to my house even though I don't know if that's a thing because I have a garden and I want to see it from a window.

Like TV, only with flowers and butterflies.

In other words, children's TV.

The garden room is attached to the kitchen and since it needed a door, the oven and cabinets had to be moved, and in any event, you see where this is going. Adding a garden room meant that a section of the kitchen got remodeled. Because the thighbone is connected to the leg bone and the leg bone is connected to the wallet.

Anybody who's ever started home improvement knows that as soon as you improve one thing, you have to improve other things, so that everything is New and Improved, like detergent, only much more costly.

But I'm not complaining.

I feel lucky to be able to make these changes, and since I work at home, I'm spending twenty-four/seven on the premises, I want the premises to suit me. And while we're turning that frown upside down, let me add that since I'm still terribly single, it's great to have everything exactly the way I want.

Finally.

And then I'll die.

My epitaph will read:

HERE LIES LISA SCOTTOLINE

DID SHE IMPROVE ENOUGH?

To stay on point, remodeling the kitchen means that I'm starting to look hard at my priorities, namely, spices. Please tell me that I'm not on the only woman who owns approximately 75,932 spices, accumulated over decades, and that the spices are dusted off every decade, which is the only time they're even touched.

I'm looking at you, cardamom.

How this came about is that when I moved the oven, I lost the shelf above it, which is where I kept the aforementioned spices, and that meant that I had to find the spices a new home or concede the obvious and throw them out.

So I began to cast a skeptical eye at my spice rack.

And it took me on a tour of my own life.

Let's begin with Marriage Rookie Enthusiasm.

In that time period of my life, I had just married Thing Two, my daughter Francesca was young and I had two stepdaughters living at home. I wanted to be not only the best mother of all time, but also the best stepmother, so I instantly bought American Mom spices, which you use when you bake apple pie. You know the autumnal array of allspice, cinnamon, nutmeg, and cloves.

I made exactly one apple pie.

Divorce ensued, but I got custody of the spices.

Then it was just Francesca and me, and being Italian-American, I decided that I was going to make homemade tomato sauce, or gravy. Mother Mary made the best gravy ever, but she refused to give me the recipe because I was a lawyer.

Don't ask.

I watched her do it and she always used onion salt, garlic salt, salt salt, and extra salt.

No fresh spices were involved.

Yet it was delicious.

Still, I could never make gravy as good as she did, and in time I gave up, though I still have the garlic salt. I feel certain that Mother Mary approves, smiling down from heaven and hoping that the garlic salt has solidified into a sodium bullet.

The next stage of my spice life was Francesca going to college, and that was when I decided I wasn't going to act mopey because I was an empty nester, and believe me, I got over that fast.

LOL.

But in spice terms, that was the time of my Indian Awakening, an idea I got from a Williams Sonoma catalogue. I bought every Indian spice known to man, extending well beyond starter curry into garam masala, turmeric, and vadouvan. They came in round pots full of orange and yellow powders, like nightmare blusher.

These were the coolest spices ever, but I never looked at them again because as an empty nester, I stopped cooking altogether.

Which was coolest of all.

This brings us to the present day, when the only spices I use are salt and pepper.

They require neither shelf, rack, nor cabinet.

They're sitting alone together on the kitchen island, like survivors of a suburban shipwreck.

Where they'll stay until the next Williams Sonoma catalogue comes in the mail.

Legends of the Fall

Lisa

My friends used to tell me, when you fall, you fall hard.
They were talking about love.

But they're not anymore.

I still fall hard, but this week it wasn't about love.

It was one of those little things that turns out to be a bigger thing, at least for me. I find life lessons in everything because I miss Oprah.

To give you some background, this is what is happening in my life right now:

The end of September is the deadline for my next book, construction on the new garden room, and my Eleventh Annual Book Club Party, for which one thousand two hundred book-club members will be coming through my house.

Honestly, I'm not complaining. I like when things are hopping, but the problem is, so was I, literally.

I was trying to hop over one of those indoor dog gates, and at the time, I was carrying a jar full of dog biscuits.

Can we pause to reflect on what a great dog mom I am?

Not only do I have stupid gates all over my house, but my

errand was making sure that the dogs not be without their biscuits for one whole minute.

Somebody must've put the dog cookie jar in the dining room, so I had to fetch it.

I'm the only one in my house who fetches.

The dogs sit on the couch and wait for room service.

Anyway, I was bringing back the dog cookie jar and hopping over the dog gate when I tripped and went flying.

For a brief moment I felt like Superwoman, but I landed like Wile E. Coyote.

I fell flat on the hardwood floor and miraculously, the cookie jar did not break, but the dog biscuits came tumbling out. The dogs rushed immediately to my side, concerned about my health and welfare.

Okay, what really happened was that the dogs rushed immediately to my side and began eating all the biscuits.

I got up, dusted myself off, and let them lick the floor clean because who needs to sweep anything when you have five dogs.

They keep house better than I do.

But by the end of that night, my back was killing me.

Coincidentally, at the time I was reading Amy Schumer's book, *The Girl with the Lower Back Tattoo*. And I became *The Girl with the Lower Back Ache*.

I could barely walk, I couldn't bend, and I couldn't open the refrigerator door, so you know this was a catastrophe.

A catastrophe caused by dogs.

Ironic.

I went immediately to my computer and started Googling

bad medical information, which is like having a doctor who makes house calls, but is alcoholic.

I spend more time on WebMD than most people spend on online porn.

In fact, WebMD is my online porn.

Who doesn't want to date a doctor?

Anyway, I gathered all the bad medical information to arrive at my own misdiagnosis, which was either that I had muscle strain or kidney cancer.

I took the road less terrifying.

Unfortunately, the treatment for muscle strain was to ice the area immediately.

Too late.

The treatment after the ice was heat.

Now, right there, I need somebody to explain to me what it is with this hot-and-cold business. How can icing be the treatment in the first hour and heating be the treatment for the second? Maybe if we didn't spend time icing it, we wouldn't have to heat it.

In any event, since I had missed the icing window, I went directly to heating, which was more fun. I was living with ThermaCare in the daytime and a heating pad at night and trying to finish my novel, clean my construction site, and get ready for the book-club party by my deadline, by which point I was pretty sure I would be dead.

And all along, I kept thinking about falling. I started to become afraid to fall. I couldn't afford another fall. I didn't have time for a strained muscle or a broken bone. I used to worry about Mother Mary falling, and even though I'm not that old, I felt that old after because I was obsessing about falling. I started to wonder if I fell because I was rushing around trying to do too many things at once.

Then I remembered that we had been working on balance in my yoga class, yet I still have the worst balance, and it struck me that maybe that was my problem.

I don't have good balance.

I'm doing too much at once, and I need to get some balance in my life.

Literally.

Remember what I told you about the life lessons?

Ta-da!

So I resolve to get more balance in my life.

After my deadline.

Political Partisan Seeks Same

Francesca

I've become obsessed with this election.

I won't tell you whom I'm supporting—just assume I agree with you so you can get through reading this.

I stay up late reading every new article and poll, my Twitter timeline reads like the watercooler at every major newspaper and not-so-major online rag, I listen to five different political podcasts on rotation, and I watch more cable news than your grandma.

There's only one area of my life left to get the political filter:

I want a partisan boyfriend.

If any guy wants to date me before November 8, we need to agree about this election.

I'm not advocating for this, I'm merely confessing to it. To those in an interparty relationship, I tip my hat to you. You have your priorities straight.

Well, one of you does.

In general, I don't think ill of the opponent's supporters.

Everyone has different needs, perspectives, and opinions, and I respect their views.

I'm just not taking my clothes off for that view.

So until November 9, I'm friend-zoning the other team.

I need a break from the constant contentiousness, and it's so much easier if we're on the same page.

Plus, what's more attractive than a man who already admits you're right?

We can exchange eye rolls over the slanted coverage and share a laugh over all the same memes.

Forget Netflix, I want to CNN and chill.

We'll watch the debates cuddled under a cozy blanket, and he'll hold me during the scary parts. Then, when it's over, the mood will be set—either by the thrill of victory or the frisson of the impending apocalypse.

And my partisan boyfriend won't criticize that hyperbole, because he'll be right there with me.

True love is being heavily biased in your partner's favor.

I'm not the only one who feels this way. Many dating apps have offered photo filters and stickers to let you announce your fierce partisanship—but in a fun way!

My friends who don't want to turn their selfies into campaign propaganda instead mention their affiliation in their bios.

I also have friends who subsequently took it out of their bios because they received too many hateful, trolling messages from fans of the other candidate.

Women on dating apps expect to be harassed with lewd sexual come-ons, but partisan insults?

Please, have some decency.

Just as we may irrationally apply bad traits to those who disagree with us, I irrationally project good qualities onto those who share my views. I find myself Googling my favorite pundits and reporters' marital status.

Just my luck, my political crushes are gay or married. All the best pundits are taken!

(Actually, one is single, and I hope he has noticed my pointed liking of all his tweets.)

Recently, one of my friends helped host a fund-raiser for our candidate. I went to support the cause and take advantage of the target-rich environment for finding the ideologue of my dreams.

I dressed as hot as is acceptable for the politically conscious. I aspired to look like *Scandal*'s Olivia Pope during Sweeps Week.

Through my political beer-goggles, all the men there were attractive. They seemed smarter, more sensitive and thoughtful than most. I knew they respected me and my opinions, and I appreciated that. What better foundation for a relationship than shared goals and worldviews?

And, wow, donating to a political campaign? That showed they cared about others and had disposable income. I was impressed.

And I hadn't even talked to one yet.

Knowing we had at least one thing in common, I was more outgoing. I struck up a conversation with a well-dressed, sophisticated man standing by the cheese plate. We got to talking about campaign strategy.

And at some point, through my fog of preapproval, I noticed he was lecturing me. He seemed to think he knew exactly what our candidate should do. He asked me only rhetorical questions to set up his next point. And he didn't ask my opinion at all.

I guess he thought he didn't have to.

I practiced my debate-podium smile as he speechified, but I was thinking he didn't look sophisticated as much as he looked too old for me. He seemed more capable of pedantry than insight. I wondered if he was ever going to stop talking.

Where's a good moderator when you need him?

Eventually, I escaped to the bar.

Election Day can't come soon enough.

Twelve Hundred of My Closest Friends

Lisa

I have good news to report for the world.

People are awesome and getting even better.

How do I know this?

Because of a completely unscientific study conducted every October at my house, in the form of a massive party for complete and total strangers.

Here's how it works.

As you may know, when I'm not writing fun stories like these, I write novels that involve murder, mayhem, and the Philadelphia suburbs.

They're fictional.

Allegedly.

Specifically, I write three books a year; a standalone that published in April, one of these fun books with Francesca in July, and an installment in the Rosato & DiNunzio series, which comes out in August.

I'm the Jekyll and Hyde of authors.

Dark Lisa writes thrillers, and Light Lisa writes jokes.

So whatever your mood, read me.

I can make you happy or homicidal.

Just ask Thing One or Thing Two.

I'm happy to say that book clubs read my books, so to encourage and reward such exemplary behavior, Francesca and I host a party in October for book clubs who have read my last April book. The party is at my house, since Mother Mary taught me that the best way to show people that you care about them is to have them over and feed them carbohydrates.

We started the party eleven years ago, when only one hundred people came.

My favorite weekend of the year!

Only.

Now we've grown to a two-day party, with six hundred book club members each day.

That's one thousand two hundred guests total, which is approximately 20,283,829,012,938,383 carbohydrates.

I live on a farm, so I have plenty of room to accommodate everyone, except for my dogs and cats, who are imprisoned in various bedrooms for the weekend. Francesca's dog Pip is permitted at the party, since he's the only one with manners, obviously because he has a better mother.

To get to my point, if you invite six hundred people to your house, the only way to greet them properly is to hug them.

I'm a hugger.

So is Francesca.

And what that means, in terms of the book-club party, is that we hug every guest when he or she arrives.

By the way, men come to the book-club party, too.

I personally enjoy hugging them very much.

But they don't smell as good as the women, who are positively fragrant.

Now in terms of my unscientific study, I am here to report to you that eleven years ago, when I started hugging unsuspecting book-club members, they didn't know how to react. Some looked startled, others simply drew away. They weren't expecting to be hugged by a complete stranger, which is a thoroughly reasonable expectation. Plus they'd read only the Dark Lisa books, so they didn't know what to do when Light Lisa tackled them with love.

There were plenty of Awkward Hugs.

An Awkward Hug is the worst thing ever. You know how it goes, one person is the hugger and the other person gasps for oxygen.

I've had marriages that were one long Awkward Hug.

Boy, bye.

But over the years, I've noticed that people at the book-club party have started hugging back, and not only that, they want to be hugged. In fact, our most recent book-club party was this past weekend, and many book-club members said, "Where's my hug?"

And these weren't people who had been to the book-club party before, but were book-club-party virgins.

They had never met me or Francesca, but they were happy to be hugged, and we all hugged each other like crazy.

And I'm telling you, this is a change that I have seen over eleven years.

Either we need more love or we're giving more love, but either way, this is a miraculous and wonderful improvement for all mankind, womankind, and book kind.

By the way, if you're wondering how long it takes to hug six hundred people, the answer is, two and a half hours. That means I got and gave five hours of hugs this past weekend, and I'm betting it will add five hours to my life.

And seriously folks, if you ask me the reason that I not only read books but write them, it's to connect with people. That's the highest and best purpose of the arts, and I believe there is nurturance, happiness, and love in that human connection. Book clubs are a way for people to connect to each other through a book, forming a soul-to-soul bond that can become a friendship lasting ten, twenty, and even thirty years.

I've seen it happen, and if you're in a book club and you agree with me, let me hear from you.

And if you're not in a book club, why not start one?

Then come over my house and get a hug.

Love is better than hate, at all times.

Running on Empty

Francesca

I don't think my body was made for running.

I took a human evolution class in college, and the professor presented his theory that early humans evolved as a species because our bodies were uniquely suited to long-distance running. Our quick-cooling slender body shape, our flexible cervical spine keeping our heads steady with our body in motion, and other traits allowed us to successfully hunt large prey animals, like zebras, by simply chasing them for long distances in the hot sun until they collapsed from exhaustion.

I must've descended from the zebras.

My body type as a little girl was the sort that made people say, unprompted, "Kids grow out, then up."

They were mostly right, but I could've used some extra inches up.

I wasn't unathletic. I was very into horseback riding, the only sport you can do sitting down.

But running has always been a slog. I used to dread the mile test in gym class. I'd try my hardest, but my lungs would burn, my sides quickly cramping with a stitch.

Yet every spring, I make a halfhearted attempt to get into running. I long to be one of those people who *craves* a run. I want the trim body, the quick calorie burn, the endorphin rush.

You know, the results.

But after a winter of hunkering down on various deadlines and letting my fitness go by the wayside—and a little on the backside, but I'm most bothered by the middle frontside—I decided I had to just do it! I would learn to love running through sheer will.

First, I tried to buy enthusiasm. I ordered new, custom-colored Nike sneakers to trick myself into getting excited about cardio.

I went for an inaugural run, full of optimism.

But even my optimism was out of shape.

After a half hour, my left knee hurt so badly I could barely walk home.

Everyone said I probably had the wrong sneakers.

The wrong, unreturnable, custom sneakers.

So I went to a running store called Jackrabbit, another animal better suited to running than I am. I brought my dog Pip for moral support.

The salesman asked me to jog on a treadmill while he filmed my feet in order to analyze my stride. He held on to Pip's leash while I did so.

As soon as I began to run, Pip lost his mind. My normally mellow pup barked his head off as if the treadmill were trying to kill me.

I always said he was smart.

The salesman showed me the video, shaky as it was thanks

to Pip's freak-out, but even I could see my ankle collapsing inward with every step.

He shook his head and informed me that I'm a serious "over-pronator."

In addition to my wonky stride, my arches are too high, and I run slightly duck-toed, all of which adds to my knee pain.

Over a hundred dollars later, I was the new owner of bulky stability sneakers, advanced orthotic inserts, and an inferiority complex.

How is it possible that I'm so naturally bad at my species' seminal advantage?

Maybe my running genes have been watered down by my Italian heritage, generations of breeding that favors painting, writing, and other butt-based activities.

Italian cardio is mostly wild gesticulation.

Our endurance is judged by one's ability to stand in a hot kitchen.

I once fried sixty-five meatballs in a galley kitchen in July using only a ten-inch pan. Where is my medal?

But that's my background; the American in me is a relentless striver.

So I'm lacing up for another miserable run.

Here's hoping I can evolve.

If You're a Woman, They Only Want One Thing

Lisa

We're having a moment, this election season.

By we, I'm talking about Women in the Philadelphia suburbs.

Like me.

I live in the Philadelphia suburbs.

In fact, it's all about me.

These days, you cannot turn on a TV channel, listen to the radio, or read an article online without hearing about whether one of the political candidates will get the vote of the Woman in the Philadelphia suburbs.

MEEEEEEEE!

I don't know how this started, but probably with political pundit Chris Matthews, who's from the Philadelphia suburbs, and Jake Tapper, who's also from the Philadelphia suburbs, and Michael Smerconish, who's not only from the Philadelphia suburbs, but still lives in the Philadelphia Suburbs.

Okay, full disclosure, Smerconish once had his book club read my latest book and he also nicknamed me Hottoline.

That's right, me.

Hot.

It was a long time ago, okay?

I cleaned up well, back then.

When I actually cleaned up.

Anyway, with the spotlight being on Women in the Philadelphia Suburbs, the candidates and their celebrity surrogates visit here all the time.

It's swinging to be in a swing state.

And the political commercials are nonstop. Some people don't like them, but I do. Especially since my other choice is a catheter commercial.

Plus my phone is ringing off the hook.

I keep hoping it's Bradley Cooper, but it's not.

He has my cell phone.

And my heart.

To stay on point, the calls come on my landline, which is a giveaway for robocallers and other calls that I ignore.

But not in election season.

Pollsters are calling to ask questions about the election, and I take the call. I answer every question they have. I yap and yap about my views. In the beginning of our phone conversation, they love talking to me. They're so used to being abused that they keep asking me questions, and I keep answering.

Then they can't shut me up.

They try to say good-bye, but I won't let them.

I talk and talk and talk.

In the end, they hang up on me.

I make them sorry they ever called a Woman from the Philadelphia Suburbs.

I turn the table.

The kitchen table.

Heh heh.

Why do I do this?

Because I might never get another chance.

Because it's taken too damn long for anybody to care what suburban women think, whether they live in the Philadelphia, Cleveland, New York, Los Angeles, Boston, Atlanta, Dallas, or any other suburb.

Because we've heard ourselves called soccer moms, hockey moms, dance moms, and every other kind of mom, whether our kids play any sport or whether we're moms at all. Because we're not considered, much less considered individuals. We've heard ourselves talked about, but never talked to, and more importantly, listened to.

We're women, constituting over half of the population of the United States, and we should count more than we have in the past.

Because even though we're marketed to for purchases from backpacks to eyeliner, boob jobs to liquor, we're rarely asked what we think.

And when we answer, nobody listens.

And if they listen, nothing changes.

So I hope that women in whichever suburbs—as well as women in the cities or exurbs—will finally get some attention. I hope that people will finally care about what we think, even if they never have before, in our lifetime.

Maybe we shouldn't be picky. We're used to being wanted for our bodies. It's an improvement to be wanted for our votes.

Plus you have to start somewhere. It's almost a century after we got the vote, and they just realized we have one.

Better late than never?

So whichever political candidate you support, I encourage you to vote.

Especially if you have ovaries.

Or used to.

I believe I still have ovaries, but I'm dead below the waist. They're there, like my appendix. Cute, but extra weight.

I can't wait to vote and I'm enthusiastic about my candidate. I hope you feel the same way about yours. But if you don't, I hope you feel enthusiastic about voting, because it matters, now more than ever. Our great country stands strong, as one of the world's most stable democracies, founded on wonderful ideals and freedoms for each and every one of us.

So show whoever's listening—even momentarily—that women have enormous political power, market power, and personal power.

It's time for them to hear us roar.

It's time for them to hear us, at all.

Mother Mary Gets an Idea

Lisa

Certain smells bring back memories of Mother Mary.

Among these are Estée Lauder Youth Dew perfume, More 100s cigarette smoke—and mozzarella.

Not exactly sentimental, but there you have it.

You can trust that all the memories of The Flying Scottolines will relate to carbohydrates.

Let me explain.

The other day, I was walking through the food court in the mall and I caught a whiff of a distinctive aroma.

Bad pizza.

Specifically, frozen pizza.

By way of background, my mother was a terrific cook, especially of Italian food. She made us homemade spaghetti, ravioli, and gnocchi from scratch. As a child, I'd spend hours watching her.

And it took hours.

If you've ever watched anybody make homemade spaghetti, it's a domestic miracle. A loaf of dough that somehow ends up being rolled out and then fed into a spaghetti maker, coming out like flour-y tinsel.

Same with ravioli, because she mixed the ricotta cheese and seasonings according to her own secret recipe that had a tangy cheesy salty taste I could never duplicate and wouldn't even try.

And when she made gnocchi, she started with the dough, but rolled it out into long, skinny tubes, cut it into little chunks, then floured her fingers and pinched each chunk, making the special dimpling that marks the best gnocchi— made by hand, dimpled by fingertips.

The problem was pizza.

When we were growing up, I wanted to be like the other kids, who got pizza delivered or had somebody go pick up pizza and brought it home. We never did that, because Mother Mary felt that since it was Italian food, it would be heresy to buy it at a restaurant. But she had no interest in making home-made pizza, and who could blame her, so she would buy it frozen at the Acme.

Or as we say in South Philly, the Ac-a-me.

She bought a no-name brand in a plastic bag, with ten small pizzas stacked on each other, as appetizing as hockey pucks.

She cooked it at home.

For three hours.

Okay, I'm exaggerating, but she overcooked the pizza every time, refusing to follow the directions. She wouldn't even let me follow the directions. It was her kitchen, so she did the cooking, which meant that our pizza always sucked.

And let's be real, back then, it was the dark ages of frozen pizza.

In fairness to Mother Mary, overcooking was the only

chance that frozen pizza had of drying out, otherwise the crust stayed soggy and the tomato sauce distilled to hot ketchup.

So as I entered high school, I ended up at a friend's house and they ordered pizza from a great neighborhood pizza place, Marrone's.

I was hooked.

So one night, when Mother Mary wanted to make frozen pizza, I told her about the magic of store-bought pizza at Marrone's, but she wasn't having any. We fussed about it, but amazingly I persuaded her to give it a try.

Mother Mary was delightfully stubborn. You could move the Mummers up Broad Street easier.

So I went to Marrone's, bought an actual take-out pizza, and brought it home.

Mother Mary opened the box, and we all waited in suspense while she slid out the first piece and cut the mozzarella strings with the gravity of a surgeon severing an umbilical cord. She took a bite, chewed, swallowed, then said with a wink:

"I knew it would be better than frozen."

From that day forward, we ordered from Marrone's.

And I forgot all about that story until I walked through the mall the other day, and smelled the mozzarella.

I knew that somewhere, Mother Mary was winking.

Grief is funny that way, bringing back the good and the bad, the funny foods and the dumb fights.

And most of all, the love.

That never goes away.

And the best of it is homemade.

Picture Imperfect

Francesca

My best friend has been living in London for the last four years, and I've been dying to visit. In preparation, I've been saving my money, browsing TripAdvisor.com, and drinking enough Earl Grey tea to earn a title myself.

Thank goodness I checked one more thing before buying my ticket:

My passport.

Expired.

Like, three years expired.

I don't know why I was surprised; I got it when I was seventeen.

I'm forever twenty-seven in my mind.

It's no great loss, my old passport photo was horrible. Caught in midblink, my eyelids are half-mast, so I look, in a very official capacity, sloshed.

The photo came at an unfortunate time about a year after my lone, teenage-rebel subversive act—a pixie haircut.

You know you're a goody two-shoes when the most rebellious act of your teen years is accidentally getting a butch hairstyle.

My old passport photo—believe it or not, taken sober

As any woman who has cut her hair very short knows, some stages of the growing-out process are better than others.

The stage captured in this passport photo can best be described as Gene Wilder.

I could only go up from here.

I'm not particularly photogenic to begin with, but I seem to strike out with every government ID.

Just once, I'd like to have a bar bouncer look at my ID without giving me that look, a disbelieving frown, like, *really*?

Yes, *really*, it's me, okay? Makeup is magic.

I watch YouTube makeup tutorials to help me fall asleep. You don't know contouring until you watch a drag queen do it.

The only compliment I've ever gotten on my license was a long-past one, when the woman who took it at the DMV handed it to me, and said, "You've got a face for the soaps."

Looking like a D-list daytime TV actress was my peak.

Unless she meant regular soap.

We're spoiled now with so many photo-filtering apps. Blemishes and lines get smoothed out, color adjusted, add a flower crown for panache.

I haven't had to post a photo of what I actually look like in some time.

All ID photos use the Mug-shot filter.

Not to be confused with the equally horrifying, Ladies Room at Work and Bathing Suit Dressing Room filters.

Around the same time I realized I needed to renew my passport, the late, great Prince came out with his, which looked like an Annie Leibovitz portrait.

I felt inspired—this was my year to step it up.

Passports are valid for ten years. This photo is going to stick with me for a while.

I don't want to pull my passport out for my romantic honeymoon and have my new husband give me the bar bouncer look:

Really?

Yes, *really*, 'til death do us part, REALLY.

The Department of State doesn't make it easy on you. They

have weird new rules for passport photos, like you can't smile with teeth.

Although they have a point; my resting bitch face is the most true-to-life.

They also suggest that you not wear your glasses to avoid your photo being rejected.

This might make me look better in my photo.

Customs agents don't make passes at girls who wear glasses.

But as luck would have it, when the day came for me to have my new passport photo taken at the local shipping center, I was suffering from the worst winter cold I'd had all year. My nose was cherry red, my face splotchy, my eyes watery.

Am I doomed to look like a drunk in every form of government ID?

But I couldn't delay if I wanted my new passport to arrive in time for my trip. So I used every makeup trick I knew to make myself look less like an extra on *The Walking Dead*.

Somehow, I made it to the store without having to blow my nose and wipe off my pancake makeup.

Actually, I do know how—I stuffed tissues up my nose like a prizefighter and covered my face with a scarf, so I wouldn't scare the neighborhood kids.

When I told the clerk I needed a passport photo taken, I thought they would take me in a little room. Instead, he just came out from behind the front counter with a bulky old digital camera, and had me stand against the wall of pens and pencils for sale, facing everyone else in line.

"Here?" I asked.

"Yeah, oh wait—" He pulled a dingy, white projection

screen down from the ceiling behind me to serve as back-drop. "Ready?"

I gave a final sniffle before closing my mouth and trying to think neutral-yet-smoldering thoughts.

Mona Lisa Blue Steel.

One second later: "Okay," he said.

"That's it?"

He nodded and showed me the back of the digital camera, where I saw a brief flash of my tiny image. "Good?"

It wasn't the best photo of me, but it wasn't the worst. No one is ever going to look at an ID photo and be wowed. If it gets me across the border, that's good enough. I just wanted to blow my nose.

"It'll do."

I waited at the counter while he went to print two copies of the standard-issue two-inch-square photos.

The clerk reappeared. "That'll be twenty-four dollars."

"For two little photos?" Finally, it was my turn to shoot the look: "*Really?*"

iPhonatic

Lisa

William Wordsworth said the world is too much with us. I bet he was talking about his smartphone.

Because I have an iPhone and I'm iObsessed.

In the past, I never approved of Those People Who Are Always Looking at Their Phones, but now I have become one of Those People Who Are Always Looking at Their Phones, which is another lesson:

Judge not, lest ye be caught looking at your phone.

And what am I looking at on my phone? Not an app, or a game, but social media. Which is a euphemism, because if you're spending all of your time looking at social media, you're the most antisocial person in the tristate area.

And which social media am I looking at?

You would think it's Facebook, but it's not, if only because of the laws of Facebook. I have an author page on Facebook, on which I can post, read comments, and reply to them, but I don't get a regular feed, which might be a blessing in disguise.

Because every time I look at Facebook, everybody is smarter, better-looking, and more remarried than I am.

Facebook can be a Depression Machine.

The social media I'm looking at on my phone, almost all the time, is Twitter.

Somebody said that Facebook is the place where you lie to your friends, and Twitter is the place where you tell the truth to strangers.

Word.

But not many of them.

If you're unfamiliar with Twitter, it's a running feed of short comments, the notorious 140 characters that can make news, offer compelling articles, or make you laugh.

And it can also misinform, enrage, and make you cry.

It can bring people together when a celebrity dies, or it can pull them apart, like when they stand up for something they believe in that others disagree with.

Not a hypothetical.

Last summer, I tweeted at *Golf Digest Magazine* because it had tweeted a photo of a golfer hitting a ball into the ocean. It struck me as a terrible thing for a publication to sanction, given the amount of trash already in our seas, which kills marine life. So I tweeted as much, politely—and in an amazing turn of events, the golfer in the photo was an up-and-coming professional who went on to make a hole-in-one the very next day, in a major tournament.

Which would be my luck.

Because the golfer's fan base exploded in just one day, and every single fan saw my tweet and tweeted back at me, ignoring my point about the environment and calling me names, which for women always begin with B, C, and W.

Of course, they're wrong.

Anybody who knows me will tell you that I am a B and a C, but totally not a W.

You might be guessing that this incident cured me of my Twitter addiction, but you would be wrong.

If anything, it made me stronger.

B stands for Bulletproof.

C stands for Confident, Capable, and Cute.

Twitter is a free way for geniuses and knuckleheads alike to express themselves, a constantly refreshing comments section, for good or ill.

Which is a recipe for complete and total addiction, if you're me.

And if you're a lot of other people, too, especially in election season. Candidates and their followers are tweeting like crazy, and as I've already confessed, I'm the Woman in the Philadelphia Suburbs who is obsessed with the election.

So I'm on Twitter.

Fairly constantly.

The irony is that as addictive as Twitter is, no other company wants to buy it. Disney, Google, and Salesforce decided not to make a bid on it, which I don't understand.

I would buy Twitter in a minute.

Except that it cost $10 billion.

And all of my money is invested in a garden room.

Home Is Where the Bra Comes Off, Part 2

Lisa

Daughter Francesca once said, Home is where the bra comes off.

I have never been prouder of my daughter.

Those of you who read me regularly know that I have been hating bras forever. And those of you who see me regularly know that I put my money where my mouth is.

In other words, Mommy is running around free!

Normally this isn't a problem because I never leave the house, and now that cold weather is here, even better. Because I wear so much fleece that Francesca calls my outfits "teddy-bear clothes."

Maybe I'm not that proud of her.

In any event, when you're wearing teddy-bear clothes, nobody can tell whether you have a bra on, especially if you're middle-aged, if you follow.

And generally, a braless middle-aged woman is not being followed.

Anywhere.

So my only bra-wearing days are if I have some sort of athletic activity, which is rarely—and sometimes not even then, depending on the bounce factor. For example, I don't wear a bra when I'm bicycle-riding anymore. There's no bouncing except when you crash, which loyal readers will know I have done on occasion.

Like, seven occasions.

But lately I've remained remarkably upright, and even the disgusting sight of me riding a bicycle braless is one that nobody has to take in for too long, as we race past each other.

They're doing the racing, not me.

I'm just riding around without a bra.

Woo hoo!

I like to feel the wind in my nipple hair.

Otherwise I'm wearing a helmet.

Just not on my breasts.

Anyway, the reason I'm thinking about bras lately is that, as you may recall, I started taking yoga. And despite my earlier whining, I'm really starting to enjoy it. Of course I haven't lost a single pound, but my back doesn't hurt anymore, so I've stopped wearing my Thermacare patches, always a lovely fashion accessory.

I know, you're probably thinking that I should wear Thermacare patches on my breasts.

Wait, what?

You weren't thinking that?

Sorry.

Anyway, to stay on point, I've been wearing my old white sports bra to yoga but I'm starting to wonder why. Every time I reach up to start our Sun Salutations, my bra salutes the sun before I do. Same thing happens when we do Goddess Pose, more Godawful than Goddess. So the last time we went into Full Cobra, I went full cobra on my bra—and managed to slip it off underneath my shirt when everybody else was in Downward Dog.

Arf!

Yay!

It's all women in the class, and nobody noticed. Or if they did, they wanted to do the same thing.

So then, just when I had my no-bra-in-yoga breakthrough, I read online that the VP of Design at Under Armour said that, "Gone are those ugly, shapeless sports bras that are the feminine version of jockstraps."

Which is exactly what I own, but never mind.

When I first read the sentence I was excited, because I thought that she was going to say that we should all take our bras off.

But I was wrong.

Instead she said, "Women want fashion elements like fun colors, prints and detailing."

We do?

I'd love detailing on my car, but on a sports bra, I'm okay with girl jockstrap.

But again, I was wrong.

The VP continued, "That's where the back detailing comes in. You need the front to be relatively around the same form so that it does its job and doesn't expose the girls . . ."

Okay, can we just stop there a moment? Breasts aren't girls. Girls have breasts. I took AP Bio, so I know.

The VP continued, ". . . so the back is really the only spot on the bra where you can have a little fun. It's all about the back!"

Which would explain why all of the new sports bras have more back straps than a parachute. But to me it seems more restrictive, not less, and it makes no sense to have straps in back, where your breasts are not.

Again, AP bio.

Ask me anything.

Fallopian tubes look like moose antlers.

I'm a font of reproductive wisdom.

Plus, who wants a sports bra with back straps that divide your back fat like a pizza?

Also quoted in the article was the chief retail analyst at the NPD Group, who said: "What you used to do was hide your underwear. Now it's no longer underwear, it's outerwear and you're being judged by it."

So for that, I have a solution.

No underwear.

On Guyatus

Francesca

I'm on a hiatus from men, a *guyatus*, if you will.

I'm taking a break from the man-hunt to focus on my writing and certain professional goals, maybe three to six months to finish revisions to my novel.

I was single before I decided to make it official, but the intentionality of it was so freeing.

It meant giving myself a break from feeling guilty for turning down a party invite just because some single guys *might* be there.

It meant taking the daunting task of making an OK Cupid, Hinge, and Match.com profile off my plate.

It meant giving myself over to the universe. If a great man fell into my lap in some stroke of Rom-Com serendipity, I'd be open to it.

But until then, I have work to do.

No biggie, right?

That's what I thought.

But I can tell I'm freaking people out. It's as if I'm swearing off men for life.

A family friend learned I was single and asked, "So, you're seeking male companionship?"

Such quaint, pre-Craigslist skeeziness in that phrase.

"I'm single, but I'm not actively looking at the moment."

Her eyes narrowed. "And how old are you?"

"Thirty." Thirty years younger than you.

She flared her eyes at me.

I tried not to roll mine.

Sometimes it gets to me. An older woman whose career I really admired admonished me, "You girls need to apply the same ambition and focus to finding a husband as you do to your careers. Otherwise, you wake up at thirty-five, and it's too late."

It broke my heart a little. Not that I was blowing my husband chances, but that a woman who built a successful career and family over decades thought thirty-five was too late for anything.

I suppose I understand this perspective from older women—they grew up in a different time! But when women my age do it to me, it bums me out.

I was at a childhood friend's bridal shower, seated with her law-school friends, nearly all of whom were engaged or married. Somehow it came up that I was single, and the very next question was:

"What are you on?"

I frowned in confusion, not realizing the correct answer was: not enough drugs to get this party going.

She clarified. "I mean, what apps?"

They have an app for drugs?

When I told her I wasn't on any dating websites or apps, she looked appalled.

"You're not doing *anything*?"

I lost my nerve. They succeeded in making me feel embarrassed about it, so I defaulted to my usual defense mechanism: humor. I launched into a one-woman show about all the terrible first dates I've been on, embellished here and there.

I killed. Had 'em rolling in the aisles.

Catching her breath, one girl exclaimed, "God, I'm so glad I'm not dating anymore. I mean, no offense."

I smiled.

Turns out you can feel cheap even without a bad date!

I was mad at myself. I'm not ashamed of being single, I have a lot of great things going on in my life without a man, why couldn't I own it?

Being single is a status, it's not an urgent problem in need of remediation.

I say "I'm single," and it's like people hear, "I have a broken faucet."

What are you going to do about it?

Have you looked online?

Can you call someone?

Sticking with my home analogy, being single should be like, "I have green shutters."

Do you want green shutters forever?

Maybe, maybe not, but they're all right for now.

When did finding love become a homework assignment?

Whatever happened to "You Can't Hurry Love"?

I thought it was good not to try too hard.

Is it only bad because I'm not trying on purpose?

Men put their love lives on hold for professional ambition all the time.

Is it because I'm a woman?

I genuinely wonder if men get this sort of reaction for being too busy to date. To a certain degree, I'm sure all benevolent-auntie types pressure young single people of both sexes to settle down.

They're equal-opportunity single-shamers.

But there's a degree of alarm when we talk to women about finding a partner that is totally unwarranted.

All single women are not miserable, or even in danger of being miserable.

Big dreams are not the exclusive province of men. Women too have great curiosity, and passion, and ambition that demand to be explored.

Go into any law school, medical school, or art school, and see the notably not-sad young women there. They're busy training themselves for the life of their dreams.

Think it's only the young women with time to spare? Stop by a small business, a research lab, the kitchen in a fine restaurant, and see women of all ages engrossed with work that means something to them.

Look in my window on a Saturday night and see me at my desk, lit by the glow of the computer screen.

I'm not in my bathrobe, weeping into a pint of ice cream, wishing a boy would call.

I'm thinking. Considering the emotions of a character I created, puzzling out a plot point in a world of my own making, perfecting the rhythm of the words in a sentence.

I'm not getting paid for it. I'm there because I want to be. And there's nothing radical about it.

I'm just a person working hard on something I care deeply about.

That's love.

Suburban Story

Lisa

I used to live in the city, but I've become completely suburban

You know how I know?

I'm obsessed with my driveway.

And I blame it all on *Downton Abbey*.

Which is not exactly suburban, but I'm getting ahead of myself.

We begin back in my days when I lived in Center City, Philadelphia, and of course I didn't have a parking space. I'd drive around the block for hours trying to find a place to park, and when Francesca was a baby, I got ticketed for pulling up in front of my own house to unload groceries, even though I lived on a side street and traffic was nonexistent.

I remember the incident to this day, mainly because when I came out of the house with Baby Francesca and found the ticket on my windshield, I cursed for a long time, which was her introduction to her mother's incredible way with words.

Later, she actually repeated one of the words, unprintable here.

Unfortunately, she's a fast learner.

Anyway, that's when my life became all about the parking.

I eventually moved out to the suburbs, where I had my very own driveway, which was a remarkable thing. It was small, but I had only one car and the driveway's size made it cheap to reseal. Then I moved down to the farther suburbs and my driveway got bigger, and it was cracking, pitting, and fading, which meant it was time to reseal.

So I got an estimate and almost fell over.

But not in the driveway, because it would've been too expensive.

My head would've made a dent that would've cost several thousand dollars to repair.

Now listen, I don't mind paying for home improvements, which is now my hobby. As we speak, my retirement fund is being invested in a garden room with copper light fixtures, cedar shakes, and a pretty turquoise couch.

But those are fun things to spend money on.

A driveway is not.

A driveway is like a black river running by your house, like a nightmare water view.

The more I started looking at my driveway, the more I started hating on my driveway.

I start to wonder if I could do anything to improve it, and then I thought back to *Downton Abbey*, which was where I get all my decorating ideas.

In my mind, that is.

I loved the TV show, but in truth, I don't remember a thing about the plot, all I recall is every inch of that incredible house, Downton Abbey.

I imagined myself living there with about three hundred dogs and an incontinent corgi.

In other words, DooDoo Abbey.

And one of the things I remembered most about Downton Abbey was the fabulous driveway.

Correct me if I'm wrong, but I seem to think it was of perfect little yellow round stones the exact color of 14 karat gold.

Like golden pebbles.

And they made a wonderfully pretentious crunching sound when one of the shiny cars drove over the driveway or one of the shiny horses clip-clopped past.

WANT.

And last summer, when Francesca and I were driving around on book tour, we ended up in beach towns, and I started to notice that the driveways were of really pretty stones, pebbles, or seashells, all of which was more appealing than my Black Asphalt River.

So when I came home, while I was running errands I started looking at people's driveways and even visited one I liked a lot, of flat red stones.

I stalked driveways.

That's pretty suburban.

I even started taking pictures of the nicer driveways and would look through them in bed at night, like pornography for middle-aged women.

Who also happen to be *Downton Abbey* fans.

There may be some overlap here.

I started calling driveway people, none of whom had heard of Downton Abbey because they lacked estrogen.

But one of them knew what I was talking about, and he talked me out of the golden pebbles because apparently they roll too much and have to be raked every day, which is perfect if you have a staff of servants but otherwise not.

Instead, he suggested that we do something called chip and tar.

Which I kept confusing with fish and chips, because it's always about the carbohydrates.

The bottom line is that they come to your house, spray goopy tar all over your driveway, then throw a bunch of tan stones on top of that.

I was sold.

And that's what we did.

It was even cheaper than another asphalt river.

And it looks fabulous.

Granted, Downton Abbey it ain't.

But I actually look forward to driving out of my house so I can hear the satisfying crunch under my tires, knowing that I am running over my retirement fund.

That's a great thing about home improvements.

You can actually see what you're mortgaging your future for.

And if you're lucky, you can hear it too.

I Like Big Brains and I Cannot Lie

Lisa

I have excellent news, ladies.

And it's excellent news for men too, depending on how they feel about big butts on women.

But, men, whatever your opinion, I'm advising you to keep it to yourself. Don't go spouting off to your wife or significant other while you're reading. You will start a conversation that can go sideways pretty quick.

Or more appropriately, south.

Bottom line, no pun, I came across an article reporting that women with big butts are less likely to develop disease and are even smarter than women with average or smaller butts.

Finally, some good news!

Even if it does seem completely unbelievable!

According to the article, women with bigger butts have lower cholesterol levels because their—correction, *our*—hormones process sugar faster. And we also have less of a risk of developing cardiovascular conditions or diabetes.

I know that sounds totally wrong, but I read it on the Internet, so you know it's 100 percent correct.

When it comes to medical information, the Internet is always dead-on.

But if you rely on it, you end up dead.

Just kidding.

I absolutely do rely on the Internet for medical advice. In fact, I don't even know why we have doctors anymore.

Oh, right, we don't.

Because if your deductible is $6500, like mine, you basically don't have a doctor. Or you better hope that if something bad happens to you, it ends up being really catastrophic so you get your money's worth.

Fingers crossed?

To return to point, the article said that women with big butts have a surplus of omega-3 fatty acids.

Or fatty assets.

Or a fatty ass.

Anyway, I believe that. Because I'm a woman with a big butt and I have a surplus of everything.

Including goodwill and happiness!

And in even better news, omega-3 fatty acids are related to improved brain function.

How great is that?

Aren't you glad you came?

You can thank me anytime!

In fact, I hope you're sitting on your nice big butt as you read this column, and now you know that you're comprehending it at warp speed because of your superior brain function.

Who knew that your brain was connected to your butt?

Unless you're one of those people who have their head up their ass.

The article even said that the fatty tissue in our butts "traps harmful fatty particles and prevents cardiovascular disease."

Wait, what?

That's basically saying that fat traps fat—but maybe it does!

After all, birds of a feather flock together.

Who are we to question Dr. Internet?

More excellent medical advice!

So from now on, just look at your big fat butt and visualize it as some extremely fleshy Venus fly-trap, trapping all the fat in the tristate area, strengthening your heart and increasing your IQ.

Fat is genius!

Now, if the medical advice in this article is true, that would mean that the Kardashians are the smartest people ever.

Laugh away, but the joke's on you.

They made zillions of dollars selling pictures of their butts.

And we bought them.

In other words, they made asses out of us.

With their asses.

GENIUS!

I must say that I have never weighed in, again no pun, on the whole big-butt phenomenon. My butt is big and always has been, but I never viewed it as positive. When I was growing up, the cool thing was to have a flat, skinny, or nonexistent butt. Happily, those days are over.

Or behind us.

Nowadays, people pay to have butt implants, and since this article, I finally understand why.

So people will think they're smart.

High Note

Francesca

Think back to yourself at fifteen.

What was your greatest desire?

What was your greatest fear?

Do you still want what you wanted then? Do you still fear what you feared?

That would be silly, right? But some of these old wishes and old dragons stick around.

When I was fifteen, what I wanted more than anything was the lead role in the spring musical, Gilbert & Sullivan's *The Mikado*.

I've written before about my long-standing, deeply nerdy love of all things Gilbert & Sullivan, and I was the only one in our drama guild who was familiar with the show when they announced it. The older girls only wanted to be the lead for the lead's sake.

I wanted to sing Yum-Yum because I loved her.

Even with this head start, it would've been quite a coup for a sophomore to nab the principal female role. So I practiced endlessly for the audition. I didn't need the sheet music that trembled in my hand.

But it was a near miss. I was cast as the understudy. And as any understudy knows, a meteor would have to strike the lead for me to get to perform.

I never did.

Which wasn't entirely bad, because my greatest fear?

Performing the lead role of Gilbert & Sullivan's *The Mikado*.

See, there's this high note in the soprano's signature aria, "The Sun Whose Rays" that scared the hell out of me. It's a B flat, not the highest note in my range, but it comes up twice, sung very slowly, and falls on the words "worth" and "a-*wake*," which are very hard words to sing so high.

When I was alone in the barn (it had the best privacy and acoustics), I could hit it most but not all of the time. But as soon as I got in front of someone, nerves clutched me around the throat, and it came out in a squeak.

The thought of missing the note in front of everyone was a recurring nightmare.

So I didn't really think I deserved the role, in spite of how much I wanted it.

Flash forward fifteen years, and the spring musical is no longer the apex of my year. Singing didn't turn out to be my truest and deepest passion simply by virtue of being the most far-fetched.

I am pursuing that passion, writing, this very minute, and I'm grateful to you readers who afford me the opportunity.

Prioritizing our pursuits is part of adult life, and not everything makes the cut. Certain interests get demoted to hobby or shelved forever. I never lose sleep over not pursuing a career in musical-theater performance.

But that doesn't mean I don't miss it from time to time.

Which is part of the reason I joined the New York Gilbert & Sullivan Society. The group isn't a performance troupe, there are other organizations that put on real productions within the communities. But that's part of why I like it—low commitment, low pressure.

I joked about it all week. How silly it was that I was doing it, how bad I was going to be with no rehearsal and being so rusty, how this was hardly some arch revenge on my high-school doubters—I ironically texted my friends:

I SHOWED THEM! LOOK WHO'S SINGING IN A CHURCH BASEMENT, BETCHES!

It was true, but it also helped me calm myself down. I couldn't admit to myself that I still cared about how this performance went.

A lot.

The night before, I allowed my thirty-year-old self one moment to take my fifteen-year-old self seriously, and I texted my friend's wife who is a voice coach to see if she had any tips on how to hit the note, downplaying it even then:

"It's a super casual concert, not prestigious. It's just that a-WAKE is such a weird sound. I have to just say, ah-WAHH."

She replied: "Minimize the W too, all you need to do is move your lips slightly to suggest the W but just stay open."

Hmm. In all my years practicing it in the shower, I had never thought of that.

When I arrived the night of the concert to see it wasn't being held in our usual church basement but in the nave of the church itself, I felt all those old nerves tightening around my throat again.

When it was my turn, I stood in the middle of the stage

and began to sing, I might as well have been a high-school sophomore again. The notes climbing slowly, higher and higher.

But then I spotted an elderly woman with white hair sitting in the audience, and I noticed she was mouthing the words as I sang them.

Maybe this was her favorite song, too, loved for a lot longer than fifteen years.

And before I knew it, the B Flat was there, and it came out, clear as a bell.

The woman clasped her hands in front of her chest when I hit it.

It was my best performance for the best audience that fifteen-year-old me could have ever hoped for.

I'm not going to make some treacly point about how it was all the sweeter for the wait. It might have meant more to me when I was fifteen, when my world was smaller, and everything felt like a big deal.

But what took me by surprise was the sense of rediscovery, of connection, and of triumph. Resurrecting that old bogeyman, defeating it, and doing something just for the love of it was well worth feeling a little silly for caring a little too much.

Life changes us.

But not that much.

Collect Them All

Lisa

You've heard the expression, "Out with the old, in with the new."

I'm not familiar.

I say that because I'm noticing lately that I'm doing a lot of "in with the new," but not "out with the old."

Maybe because I'm getting older.

Or because I'm getting wiser.

Either way, I have too many books.

I know, I don't think it's a problem, either.

The only thing is, they're overtaking my house.

We begin a few years ago, when I notice that my books are piling up all over my dining table and I didn't have any bookshelves for them. So I had some bookshelves installed, first one wall of them in the dining room, than a second wall, and a third, and over time, even those bookshelves got full. All these were books that I have read and loved, then I started collecting signed books, and so when one of my favorite authors would tour, I just called the store.

Who knew you could do that?

I did.

I started to get to the point where I shelved my signed books separately, in alphabetical order by author, and even had a little sign made for them.

The sign says, Signed.

Subtlety is not my strong suit.

You know this if you read my books.

Then my signed collection of books started growing, roughly at the same time as my TBR pile started growing. Hard-core readers know that a TBR pile means books To Be Read, but for me, it could easily mean books To Be Reshelved Without Being Read, because more and more, I am acquiring too many books.

Let's assume for present purposes there is such a thing.

And so now I'm thinking about putting more bookshelves in my kitchen, of all places.

Why?

Because it's the only room in the house that presently has no bookshelves.

I don't know if you can put bookshelves in the kitchen, or if it's against federal law, but the great thing about a middle-aged woman is that we make our own rules.

And also that we never throw anything away.

And now there are going to be bookshelves in my kitchen.

Because I can't part with a single book.

I don't even lend my books.

Why?

Because they're mine, all mine. I treasure each one. I just love books.

The child in me will ask, if you love books so much, why don't you marry them?

The answer, of course, is that I have.

I have books that lasted longer than both marriages combined, and somewhere along the line, I became a collector.

I always thought that the world divided up into people who collect things and people who don't, with me being distinctly in the latter, but no longer.

I stopped being judgy.

And somehow the pleasure from collecting is different from everything else. Maybe it's rooted in the childhood

You can never have too many books!

commercials, because I know I can recall them instantly, where they say, Collect Them All.

And here I am, collecting them all, which is the worst kind of acquisitive urge because it's one that can never be fulfilled.

I mean *all*?

It was one thing when there were three Barbies, but now there are 479 Barbies, and of course there are an endless number of books.

And I can't seem to help myself, nor do I even want to try.

My name is Lisa and I'm a bookaholic.

Please tell me I'm not alone in this.

Are any of you collecting anything? Is it threatening to overtake you? Are you building more shelves, display cases, or signs that say Signed?

Have you lost your damn mind, too?

Or are we simply greedy?

I'm wondering what drives the urge to collect, and whether it's just hoarding without a cable TV show.

What set am I trying to complete?

And don't tell me it's myself.

Because you might be right.

It's a Boy!

Lisa

Did you hear they invented a birth control that men can use?

Just kidding.

Seriously.

By way of background, you may have heard the news that recently, there was a trial of 266 men who took hormonal birth control, in the form of an injection that mixed testosterone and progestogen. An article I read said that the idea was to "trick the testicles into reducing production of the highly concentrated testosterone they need to create sperm."

Quite an idea.

Happily, my days of tricking testicles are over.

In fact, testicles might be the only thing about men I don't miss.

I bet no women like testicles.

I bet men don't like them, either.

I mean, really.

Do they own a mirror?

Anyway, to stay on point, the male hormone shots worked, because they produced a pregnancy rate of 1.57 per 100.

So apparently you can be half-pregnant.

Maybe even one-and-a half-pregnant.

This was great news for the people who ran the study, because it was the same level of effectiveness as the birth-control pill that women have been taking for decades.

So far, so good, right?

No.

The study was halted because of the side effects of the shots. I did some research into what the side effects were, and some of the men complained of moodiness and depression.

Just like female birth control.

But evidently we handle it better?

Or maybe we're not used to complaining.

Or maybe nothing happens when we do?

Or maybe, just maybe, we're more manly than the men getting testosterone shots.

Which is pretty damn manly.

But still, the news story didn't make sense to me.

So I kept digging to see what other side effects the men reported, and apparently, another one was increased libido.

Hello.

I've never known a man to complain of increased libido. Though I have known of women to complain of a man's increased libido.

Thanks, Viagra.

Since that side effect didn't make sense to me either, I kept digging, and I learned that the final side effect reported was acne.

Hmm.

I've never known a man to care if he has a zit, especially if there was a possibility of sex.

Only women think that zits make sex more unlikely.

Either way, I have a cure.

Turn out the light.

So then I dug a little more, and I found the one fact that wasn't widely reported—the injection of the hormone shot had to be "just above" the scrotum.

Now look, I admit, what I know about men can barely fill a test tube.

But I have common sense.

And my guess is that a needle in the balls was more than most men could deal with, and who can blame them?

I tried to learn online about what "just above" meant, but I expect for most men, that might be a distinction without a difference.

Notice I didn't say splitting hairs.

By the way, my research also showed that the injections were bimonthly, and I looked up whether that meant twice a month or every other month. And according to the Oxford Dictionary, it can mean either.

What?

Doesn't that make a difference?

Especially if you're the man getting a needle in his balls?

I think you might be able to turn his frown upside down if you said it was every other month.

But if it's twice a month, most men might say no, thanks.

Now that would be a side effect that would end a study.

So we have our answer.

There won't be male birth control unless we can find a better way to deliver it to men.

Like in beer.

In any event, the whole idea of men using birth control might be an exercise in be-careful-what-you-wish.

I used to think that male birth control would be a wonderful idea, but honestly, I wouldn't want to delegate my birth control to somebody else, especially a guy who always forgets where he put his car keys, socks, and phone.

After all, if he makes a mistake, only one of us is left holding the bag.

So to speak.

Remote Control Freak

Lisa

My life has just been changed.

How, you ask?

Did I win the lottery?

Did I meet a man and fall in love?

More realistically, did I get another dog?

No, I got a new remote control.

And it changed my life.

I'm still trying to decide if this means something great about me or something awful.

On the Great side of the ledger is that it's the simple things in life that matter.

On the Awful side of the ledger is that remote controls are not what they mean when they say it's the simple things in life that matter.

And actually, what I think they say is that the best things in life are free, and let me tell you, Comcast is certainly not free.

But for good or for ill, I just got married, and this time it's forever.

The deal was clinched by my new remote control, which

is the latest and greatest incarnation that the company offers, and for that, I owe thanks to you, my beloved readers.

How so?

We begin our story when I do the laundry, which happens about once a month, no kidding.

I will let my sheets rot before I wash them, mainly because ain't nobody sweating in my bed, if you follow.

You will recall that dogs don't sweat.

I hate doing the laundry and so generally I gather up the sheets and a blanket really carelessly, roll them up into a ball, and stuff them in the washing machine and get it started. Invariably, somewhere in the middle of the cycle, the machine will stop and its yellow light will blink UL, which stands for uneven load.

I'm like, you're telling me.

My load in life has been uneven for a long time.

And where can I find somebody to do mommy's laundry?

So you get the idea, I'm so careless with doing laundry that last week when I washed my sheets, I accidentally washed my TV remote, so it'll be really clean for the next time I wear it.

And if that's not dumb enough, the next time I did the sheets, I washed the remote that I replaced it with, but miraculously, it still worked after. But the point of the story is that I posted on Facebook about the miraculous remote control that worked even after it went through the washing machine, and one of you genius readers posted:

"Lisa, you have the old remote."

That was all I needed to hear.

And now I have the new remote, which not only changed my life, but renewed my faith in American ingenuity.

Uh-oh!

Number one, it only has one button to turn the TV on and off, the way God intended.

This is a little-known fact, but it was actually Satan who invented the idea that you had to press a TV button and turn that on or off, then press a Cable button and turn that on or off.

The work of the devil.

Or the cable company.

Number two, the new remote control has voice recognition,

so if you want to turn the channel to NBC, you just say, "NBC" to the remote.

In other words, you can actually talk to the remote control and have it do what you say—when you say it!

How many women have ever experienced that sensation? Not this one.

Yet another reason I'm sure this marriage will last forever.

Finally, and best of all, the remote control actually knows when it's dark out and lights up if you pick it up at night, which if you ask me, is the reason science was invented in the first place.

I remember writing long ago that I used to be jealous of Daughter Francesca's remote control in New York City, which has a button that you could turn on to light up the remote. But now, here in Philadelphia, we don't even have to press a button.

Our remote controls just *know*.

So it's a brave new world for me, and for you too, if you get this new remote.

It didn't even cost anything extra, above and beyond my normal monthly cable bill of $2,938,749,399,393.20.

Because the best things in life really are free.

The Bridal Shower 2.0

Francesca

We need to talk about bridal showers.

We've been kicking the can of this conversation down the last hundred years, and our procrastination has resulted in some stale, kinda sexist party games slipping under the radar.

Gals, we can do better.

Women used to get married a lot younger than we do now. At the turn of the century, when bridal showers first gained popularity, a woman achieved menarche and was ready for marriage.

You know the tradition is old, because they still called your period "menarche."

Back then, you packed everything you owned—a mother-of-pearl hair-comb and a couple of pairs of hand-sewn bloomers—into a bindle and walked from your dad's house to your husband's.

It was easy to throw a great party in those days. You didn't have to compete with smartphones.

Some of these bridal-shower games were amusingly quaint in the 1950s, they're getting weird for a millennial bride.

For example, we have to stop treating bridal showers like housewife job training.

A.) Keeping house isn't only a woman's job anymore, and B.) chores aren't that complicated or fun.

I've heard of a shower game where the bride is blindfolded and she has to guess the kitchen utensil by touch alone.

Unless this is prep for kinky kitchen sex, this game is past its sell-by date.

Come to think of it, that might be a great update! Blindfold the bride and have her reach into a bag to guess: sex toy OR kitchen utensil?

Hmm, is that a rolling pin or a—

Okay, maybe we'll save it for the bachelorette party.

Then there's the classic request that shower guests bring recipe cards. My friends and I love to cook, but as soon as you make it "womenfolk only," you suck the fun out of it for millennial women.

It makes me want to write, "ORDER TAKEOUT" or "WHAT'S FOR DINNER? I DUNNO, ASK HIM" in protest.

And about the card part—I never have one, I always have to make a special trip to Staples to buy a pack of three hundred index cards, and, after using one for this recipe, promptly misplace the other 299. And I'm sorry, but no woman my age has a physical recipe box.

Today's recipe box fits in your pocket and it's called the Internet.

Maybe we could email our recipes to the bride and groom, unless email is too impersonal.

But then the happy couple could store them on the Cloud along with their naked pictures.

The Cloud is the most personal.

And while old family recipes are worth passing down, older female relatives have a lot more to offer than casserole recipes. My friend's shower had a great twist they called "words of wisdom" cards, where the married women read aloud their best marital advice.

These grande dames got real.

I found myself wanting to take notes on the back of my recipe card.

Maybe I was so into it because all the women in my family have been divorced.

At my bridal shower, only those divorced *once* can offer wisdom cards.

The ones divorced twice will provide the business card of their favorite lawyer.

Just for the prenup, of course. Do you really think I'd let Pip's custody fall to litigation?

I need pre-pup.

Secondly, I completely understand the need for icebreakers among bridal-shower guests, often an intergenerational group from different families and social circles. But why are so many bridal-shower games vaguely humiliating?

As a guest, I can't say I love the toilet-paper-dress game. The one where teams of guests compete to create the best bridal gown out of toilet paper.

Toilet paper stopped being hilarious when I turned ten.

You TP the house of the neighbors you hate, you TP a wet public toilet seat, and you TP your actual butt.

Don't TP your friends.

Every gown comes out looking like a lazy Halloween costume. Toilet paper is a really difficult material to work with. I'm pretty sure there's a *Project Runway* episode to back this up.

Not to mention the awkwardness of choosing teams, then choosing the "model" bride, and finally naming one team a winner and the rest losers.

There's enough tension among the bride's friends as it is—bridesmaids vs. regular guests, Maid of Honor envy, the childhood friends and the college friends facing off like the Sharks and the Jets. We can't handle any more competition.

Although, if the games are going to put someone on the spot, I'd rather it be the guests than the bride. I once went to a shower where the bride was quizzed on trivia about her fiancé in front of everyone.

You might as well rename this the "Future In-Laws Judge the Bride" game.

I'm not a fan of quizzing the bride on anything, but if we must, let's ask her questions about the hubby that are helpful for a wife to know.

Questions like, how many drinks can he tolerate at a dinner before he puts his foot in his mouth?

Does he *really* know how to fry a whole turkey, or is he going to blow himself up in the backyard?

What's his email password?

Credit score?

At least these answers could come in handy.

Why are we giving the bride a hard time? The woman is planning a giant party to feed you expensive finger food while she herself is suffering through a yearlong pre-wedding diet. *Do not push* her right now.

Instead, let's ask the guests to play a game to see how well we know the bride. Maybe have everyone bring a favorite picture with the bride and share the memory behind it.

Flattering memories, obviously. Not spring break '07.

Never spring break '07.

This would give the groom's side of the family who might not know the bride as well valuable insight into the many wonderful facets of the bride's personality and past.

I basically want the whole shower to be one giant advertisement for the bride.

The groom's family should leave not only wanting her to marry their son, they should want her to run for office.

The purpose of the bridal shower is to celebrate the bride, and to make two different families and many groups of friends unite in support of her marriage. That's a tradition worth preserving.

And I guess, if it really means a lot to you, TP me.

House Dreams

Lisa

I finally figured out why I'm addicted to home improvement.

It's all Barbie's fault.

To give you some background, like most little girls, I had a Barbie doll. I remember her distinctly because she had a blond ponytail with weird curly bangs, red lipstick, and a strapless black-and-white bathing suit that could never stay up.

Slutty Barbie.

This was back in the days when kids only had one Barbie, but bought a bunch of different clothes for them and dressed them in different outfits.

The Dark Ages, Toy-wise.

Back when blocks were made of wood, books were made of paper, and a remote-controlled toy was one you pulled on a string.

I had a Gaylord The Walking Dog, now sold online as a vintage toy.

Oy.

Anyway, to stay on point, though I had Barbie, I didn't love her as much as I loved her house.

Who can forget Barbie's Dream House?

It was a rectangular box of turquoise cardboard that unfolded to make a layout of a living room with a cardboard console television, squarish cardboard furniture, with a cardboard pink vanity on one wall, inexplicably.

Or maybe not inexplicably, since it was Barbie's, and God knows she was vain.

Amazingly, I don't have to remember what the Barbie Dream House looked like because I got my Dream House back as an adult, and like many things in my life, it came to me through the beneficence of my readers. One day I got an email from a wonderful couple in New Jersey, saying that they had found an old Barbie Dream House at a tag sale and that my name was inside it, and to make a long story short, they gifted it to me.

And now I have my actual original Barbie Dream House.

Which needs as much work as my real house.

But I never made the connection between the Barbie Dream House and my real house until last weekend, when I got another harebrained home-improvement scheme.

To wit, I decided to paint my front door.

Maybe because the new garden room, still under construction, looks out on the flowers, which are so colorful, but whatever the reason, it started to bother me that my front door is plain white, like the front of the house. I've always liked houses that have a different color front door, so I became obsessed with the idea of doing something bold in my front door.

I even found a paint company that will sell you a paint-your-own-door kit, complete with brushes, high-lacquer paint, and a bottle of wine.

I'm only kidding about the wine.

But the question is, what color should the door be?

You may remember that I painted my shutters a yellow that turned out to be so bright I have to wear sunglasses, but mercifully, the color has faded over time, so now it's merely radioactive.

So I tried to think about what color door would go with insanely yellow shutters, and some of the choices were a lovely forest green, a cobalt blue, or even a bright red, which looked too McDonald's.

Do you want fries with that?

But then I started to think about it, and I realized a door color is probably the most important color in the house, because it's the first thing you see every time you come home. It should make you feel welcome and happy. So I asked myself, Lisa, what's your favorite color?

I chose a pink from a slew of different pinks and showed the paint chip to Daughter Francesca, who instantly said:

"That's Barbie pink."

I realized she was exactly right.

And I made the connection between the Barbie Dream House and my real house, which I'm trying desperately to turn into my dream house before I die.

So I'm painting my door Barbie pink.

Why?

Because we girls can do anything.

SuperLisa

Lisa

I wasn't born yesterday.

So I have no excuse.

But I am easily the most gullible person I know.

How do I know this?

For starters, I married Thing One and Thing Two.

But specifically today, I'm talking about believing a lot of dumb food claims, which has resulted in me buying a lot of dumb foods that fill my pantry. All I have to do is open the door and I see evidence of my own folly, staring me right in the face.

Let's begin with teff.

What? you say.

You probably don't know what teff is, and neither did I at first, which is the way it suckered me in. I have a weakness for the secret health food that I've never heard of before, with an impossibly weird name.

Like teff.

I first read about teff in an article in the newspaper, which had all the ingredients of the kind of food scam that gets me every time. Not only the incomprehensible name, but the mysterious place of origin, usually far away, if not downright exotic. In the case of teff, it is the traditional grain of Ethiopia.

Right there, I'm listening.

That's exotic.

I don't know anything about Ethiopia except that I once went to a restaurant in Philly where you ate with your hands, giving me the undoubtedly erroneous as well as racist impression that people eat with their hands in Ethiopia.

If true, God knows how they eat teff.

Because as a factual matter, at least according to the package, teff is the smallest grain in the world.

You're interested, right?

It's intriguing.

But I'm getting ahead of myself. As soon as I read the article, I went online and researched teff. I learned that it has a lot of iron, a superfood for women that was supposed to give you a lot of energy.

Energy is the key word for me, especially on deadline.

I know I'm not alone in this because people buy energy bars and energy drinks, but everybody knows those things aren't necessarily healthy. I myself usually get my energy in the form of Dunkin' Donuts coffee with extra sugar— or chocolate, which comes with all the extra sugar you need.

In other words, that's not healthy energy, either.

Plus I read that the iron in teff is especially important for women because we lose so much iron in our menstrual cycle.

Of course, that doesn't apply to menopausal women like me, who lost not only our iron but our menstrual cycle itself, but still.

Teff for all!

Some of you might be thinking that if I was on such a quest for healthy energy, I could start exercising, but let's not get crazy.

This is America, where we eat in the quest to lose weight.

Anyway, so I went to three different grocery stores, but none of them had teff. In fact, when I asked the clerk in customer service, none of them knew what teff was, and one salesperson thought I was sneezing.

But the harder it was to find, the more I wanted it.

"Supply limited" is another sales pitch that always works with me.

Of course the supply is never limited.

But you never know.

I just can't take that chance.

I'm gullible, see?

So I finally found a store that had a bag, which I opened eagerly the moment I hit the house. I'd never seen anything like teff, which is a tiny little red grain that looks like a pile of iron itself.

I could feel the energy surging through my body.

The recipes on the bag said that you could put teff in a porridge or pilaf, but I never make porridge or pilaf.

Because I'm not Ethiopian.

So I opted for boiling it for twenty minutes, until it turned into a red glop that looked like bloody mashed potatoes.

I took a forkful and it tasted vaguely nutty, then I ate the rest and waited to feel energetic.

But it didn't happen.

I'm still my lazy old self.

Maybe if I had eaten it with my hands?

Hi, My Name Is

Francesca

"It's a good networking opportunity."

If there's a more anxiety-inducing sentence than that, I don't know it.

Networking is the worst. I like people and I'm outgoing, but I like connecting with people on a real level. I have a great, internal radar for genuine, down-to-earth people and I bond with them quickly.

I make friends. I don't make "contacts."

Only sociopaths enjoy interacting with others for the purpose of using them to their professional advantage.

I was invited to a best-selling author's publishing anniversary party. The author being feted is one of the nicest in the business, and I wanted to go to celebrate him. But I knew, by virtue of it being an "industry" party, I wouldn't be allowed to just eat the cake and enjoy myself.

I'd have to network.

And I'd be flying solo. My mother was also invited, but she wasn't free. My agents hadn't been invited, but they were very eager for me to go.

They even emailed me links to the professional bios and

photos of several editors who would likely be at the party that I should try and make an impression on.

I felt like I was a spy receiving a dossier of my targets.

Only instead of charming the pants off these women, I was supposed to charm the book contracts out of them.

What's the first thing a good spy needs? A good disguise.

I scheduled a haircut for right before the party, so that my normally kinky, curly hair would look smooth and professional.

Confidence, from the outside in.

As soon as I arrived, I was greeted by a big table of name tags, and relief washed over me. I love a good name tag.

A name like Francesca Serritella hits a lot of people's ears like Fettucini-Spaghetti-ella the first time they hear it. Seeing it in writing helps.

I clipped that thing to my right boob with pride.

But once I got into the room, only about 15 percent of people were wearing theirs.

Yo, adults too cool for name tags at a professional event: get over yourself. We are all too old to be cool.

I'm only thirty, and did you hear me just use the word, "Yo?" I rest my case.

Plus, in the book world, people are best known for their words, not their image. I was terrified of embarrassing myself by failing to recognize some superfamous author.

If you pass on the name tag, maybe pin your latest book jacket to your shirt.

Scanning the room, it was like the high-school cafeteria all over again, and I had no one to sit with.

I felt painfully self-conscious when I was standing still.

I told myself, *you're a shark, you're fine as long as you keep moving.*

As I weaved through the tables, I held my head high, peering around as if I might be looking for a friend, all the while trying to catch someone's eye for an opening.

But it wasn't working. Everyone had their cliques!

The book industry is comprised of a lot of nice, normal people who work in offices, like the editors, agents, publicists, cover artists, booksellers, etc., who interact with each other often, *plus* the authors, who are hermit weirdos.

Ninety-nine percent of my professional life is conducted alone, behind a computer screen, usually eating something that drops crumbs on my lap.

I've published eight books over as many years, and I can count the number of colleagues I regularly interact with on one hand.

If book parties are high school, authors are Chess Club.

By the hors d'oeuvres, I zeroed in on a group of particularly smiley women, definitely not the mean girls' table.

They said they worked for one of the big publishing houses, and I told them I was just finishing my first novel, and lo and behold, they asked me about my book.

I launched into my elevator pitch, excitedly thinking, *oh my God, I'm doing it, I'm networking, I'm advancing my career this very minute.*

The woman seemed into it, I thought we were really clicking, until she asked me, "What are the grades?"

"I'm sorry?" I carried a 4.0 in high school . . .

"The book, what reading level is it?"

"Oh no, my book is definitely adult. Well, not, *adult*-adult, not like porn." I laughed nervously.

"We work in the children's division."

"Oh . . ." my voice raised an octave, "that's nice."

Welp, five minutes down, one hour and fifty-five minutes to go.

I was too intimidated to approach groups of four or more people. But I would hover around the smaller groups, and, if I sensed a lull, I tried to compliment my way into the conversation.

"Wow, I love your dress. Hi, I'm Francesca."

It's like a platonic, woman-to-woman pickup line.

I *oohed* and *ahhed* over so many outfits and accessories, my next career move should be on the Home Shopping Network.

I spotted a woman with the most beautiful curly hair, a pile of chestnut ringlets.

"You have to tell me what hair products you use, because your hair looks amazing."

She lit up and we started talking.

"Okay, I'm buying all this stuff," I said. "Thanks for the tips, we curly heads gotta stick together."

She smiled, but her brow furrowed. "But you don't have curly hair."

My blowout! The essential part of my please-take-me-seriously disguise. I'd completely forgotten. I explained that I don't really look like this, I just tried to change everything about myself for this event.

She laughed. I don't remember what her job was, or if there

was any purpose to our conversation, but we were buds for the rest of the party.

Next time I have to go to one of these networky things, I won't come as a spy, or a shark, or a smooth-talking salesman. I'll come as myself.

With a name tag.

Netflixxed

Lisa

I have never lived unplugged.

But I'm trying it now.

Let me explain.

I love TV, and I tend to keep it on all day long while I'm writing.

TV is my friend.

And TV is the perfect kind of friend on deadline, because it makes no requests like conversation, lunch, or a movie, but is content to play in the background of my life, an innocuous sound track of truck commercials, *Real Housewives* dilemmas, and Dr. Phil.

At my house, the doctor is always in.

Though I still miss Oprah.

She was my goddess.

I watch her channel too, but it's so good that my emotions usually get engaged, which is a no-no during first draft.

Iyanla, fix my book!

And so for a while, the perfect solution was a cable news channel. I thought it would keep me up to date on important things, but as the election got closer, I thought there were a lot of pundits who didn't know anything, wildly careless statements, rehashed speculation, and coverage better suited for the trotters at a low-rent racetrack than the presidential election of the United States of America.

The same thing happened with social media, like Twitter and Facebook. No matter which candidate you liked, I don't think any of us liked the media coverage. And it continued even after the election, which was when I finally decided to pull the plug.

Well, not completely.

I'm not insane.

Because when I got my new remotes, I happened to notice that Netflix was offered on my television.

Wow!

What a country!

I had only rarely watched Netflix before, mainly for television shows I had missed in real time, but suddenly there it was, staring me in the face.

A :-) in a pink block, with my name underneath:

lisa

How cute is that?

So I clicked and went through the torturous log-in procedure, where you spell your long Italian-American name into a bewildering seek-and-find of letters and numbers.

It's not a login, it's an IQ test.

And once you pass that, the menu isn't much easier. I had a hard time trying to find movies and TV shows, and more than once I had to resort to another seek-and-find.

Netflix, help a sister out.

But after a while, I got the hang of it, mainly because I

started with the comforting SUGGESTED FOR YOU shows.

I must admit, I like this idea.

I usually make all my decisions on my own, and though I know how lucky I am in that, I also understand why a corporate CEO will go to a dominatrix for sex.

Once in a while, it's nice to let someone else decide.

Especially if they make good decisions.

And they pay attention to your safe word.

Mine is Bradley Cooper.

So I started following the Netflix suggestions and I began to fall in love. Not just with the shows, but with Netflix. It understands me better than any man I've ever married or divorced, and not only that, it listens to me. It notices what I like and gives me more of it, as if it really cares.

Netflix, marry me?

I cannot be the first woman who's felt this way. We're such easy creatures, we females. Maybe there's an algorithm in our ovaries.

What do women want?

More of what we like and less of what we don't.

If Netflix can do it, why can't men?

So for the past week while I write, I've had on the soothing background music of every single crime drama ever produced.

In the world.

The American ones are awesome, like *Bloodline*, and I also love the ones out of the UK, like *Happy Valley* and *The Fall*. Though I admit I had to put in the subtitles to deal with the British, who clearly speak English way better than we do.

And also have a completely different vocabulary of curse words.

Bollocks!

It sounds like buttocks, but it's not.

Though I think it means the same thing.

Then I segued into *Narcos,* about Pablo Escobar and the drug cartel, which was more challenging because it uses so much Spanish that I had to study the subtitles. I knew I was in trouble when I typed *federales* into my last manuscript.

And Netflix can scratch whatever itch you have. Like in my case, I'm still in mourning over *Downton Abbey,* so I discovered *The Crown,* which features some of the most gorgeous interiors on the entire planet.

Let me just say, Buckingham Palace beats Downton Abbey, hands down.

Watch two minutes of the show, and you will get three hundred decorating ideas, none of which you can afford, including the fresh-cut flowers.

Just go with Edible Arrangements.

I wonder if the Royal Family has one of those in the kitchen and I bet they're avoiding those weird cherries, like the rest of us. You know, the ones that stain the pineapple a nice carcinogenic red.

And of course, the binge-watching thing is its own reward, and if you work eight or nine hours at a stretch, like I do, you will cover the entirety of Queen Elizabeth's reign, which is ninety years in ten episodes.

It's like dog years.

So Netflix is getting me through my final draft and the postelection season.

And at night, I read before bed, instead of watching the TV news or checking out social media.

A real book, instead of Facebook.

And you know what?

I'm happier and healthier.

Isn't that what life is all about?

The End.

Like a Rolling Book

Lisa

Bob Dylan won the 2016 Nobel Prize for Literature.

Yay?

I'm of two minds about this, which is so Dylan of me.

My initial reaction was sheer delight because I'm a huge Dylan fan.

In fact I have a major crush on him.

I have almost all of his albums and I read four books about him, including the one he wrote about himself. When I first heard that he had won, I fired off a tweet that said something like, "I'm so happy that Dylan won, all of the arts are connected!"

I know, right?

I was stating an essential truth of pageant-level depth.

Welcome to Twitter.

I do believe that all of the arts are connected, and his lyrics are poetry, and poetry is certainly literature, and the thighbone is connected to the leg bone.

Ipso facto, Dylan gets the Nobel Prize.

If you follow.

And you know how fans are. Fans get happy when their

team wins. Even if it happens because of a bad call, a fluke, or just sheer good luck.

We call that winning ugly.

But it's still winning.

And we love to win!

Go, Dylan, go!

But after the initial excitement subsided, I started to wonder if this was a good thing. I saw the reaction online from fellow authors, publishers, booksellers, librarians, and people who love books in general. And I began to think it was a shame not to award the prize for literature to a wonderful author, rumored favorites like Philip Roth or Margaret Atwood.

In college, I took a yearlong course with Philip Roth, and he's a brilliant author who made me look at literature in a whole new way.

Didn't he deserve that prize?

Yes.

Because he gave me an A.

Plus many readers, including myself, like to buy prize-winning books, and it's helpful to guide people to quality books. But now that opportunity is missed.

The Nobel Committee says they gave Dylan the prize for "having created new poetic expressions within the Great American song tradition."

But maybe it's too smart by half to award a prize in literature to songs, even a body of remarkable songs.

Songs are wonderful, but they're not novels.

I know this because I've written thirty novels, and they are each about a hundred thousand words long.

And they don't sound like anything unless you read them out loud.

You can't hum them like *Mamma Mia.*

Or stop humming them like *Mamma Mia.*

Previous winners of the Noble Prize for Literature have been Ernest Hemingway, William Faulkner, John Steinbeck, and Gabriel Garcia Marquez.

I don't know if any of those guys can sing.

But honestly, neither can Dylan.

The Nobel was established by the will of Alfred Nobel, and it awards prizes for Physics, Chemistry, Medicine, Literature, Economic Sciences, and Peace.

More STEM-heavy than I had realized.

You know what's conspicuously absent?

Music. Songs.

So what does that say about Nobel's intent in his will?

What would he, the inventor of dynamite, have wanted?

To explode the literary world?

So I started to wonder if my initial reaction had been because of my crush.

Dylan didn't say anything for several weeks after the announcement was made that he'd won this incredibly prestigious prize. The Nobel Committee tried to contact him, but was unable to, and when reporters asked him about that at a concert in Oklahoma, he answered, "Well, here I am."

Maybe the Committee couldn't get concert tickets?

And then, when he was asked if he would go to the award ceremony, he answered, "Absolutely, if at all possible."

Now he's starting to sound like my ex-husbands, Thing One and Thing Two.

I searched in vain to see if Dylan simply said, thank you.

No.

Oops.

And no word from him on the million-dollar prize, either whether he will accept it, donate it, or use it to mix up the medicine with Johnny in the basement.

But I figured out a surprise ending, a way for everyone to come out of this perfectly.

Dylan should have been given the Nobel Prize for Peace.

He has written and performed so many antiwar songs that they defined more than one generation, and his music really does build empathy worldwide and unite the entire globe.

Not a bad idea, huh?

Bob, call me.

Sniff Test

Francesca

Every woman has one department at the shopping mall that calls to them, nay, sings to them, like a choir of angels, radiating a warm, golden light from the top of the escalator.

For me, it's fragrance.

I'm hypnotized by those glittering little bottles on glass countertops, each one with a secret inside, winking at me from across the room.

I've always loved perfume, ever since I was a little girl, when the crystal bottles on my mother's dresser seemed like magical potions.

And whenever I smelled them on her, I knew she was going somewhere glamorous, mysterious, and as-yet-off-limits to me.

Douleur exquise!

Now that I am grown-up, perfumes are the closest thing I have to fairy godmothers. Scents have the power to turn me, a regular girl in dog-hair-covered yoga pants, into whatever sort of woman I want to be.

Bibbity-bobbity-spritz!

I've accumulated a lovely perfume collection of my own,

but there's always more to be explored. And the best thing about the fragrance department can be summed up in one word:

Testers.

Makeup departments have testers, but often you twist up the lipstick to find its head all deformed and tacky, maybe a stray piece of lint stuck to it, and you have to ask yourself:

"Is this going to give me herpes?"

I need more elegance than that. With perfume, you spritz the fancy cardstock, give it a limp-wristed shake, like it's a Polaroid picture you already know you look great in, and voilà! A new scent to delight or disgust you.

In fashion, if you try on a pair of jeans that look bad, you blame yourself.

In fragrance, if you try a perfume that stinks, you move on.

And boy do I move. I require a very patient salesperson, because if I get in my head that I want a jasmine scent, I will need to smell every perfume with a jasmine note in creation before I can decide.

Only the best contenders get valuable real estate on my skin. I tell myself I will pick the top two and put one on each wrist. But then I discover another great scent, so I have to find a new spot, maybe my left inner-elbow. And before I know it, I need a map of my body labeled like a butcher's chart to remember what I put where.

I know I've walked out of the fragrance department looking like I'm smelling my armpit, but really I'm revisiting the perfume I tested on my right shoulder cap.

But I can't hang out in a fragrance department all day, can I?

I asked and they said no.

So I had to find a new outlet for my insatiable curiosity. And where does one go for insatiable curiosity?

The Internet.

That's where I discovered Fragrantica.com, a website for maniacs.

It's a self-described "perfume encyclopedia" of mind-boggling dimension. It details forty thousand perfumes with over six hundred thousand reviews written by nearly half a million registered users from around the world.

In addition to user reviews, it also has industry news, blog posts, reference material, discussion forums, and something called "fragrant horoscopes."

The webpage itself is cluttered, the interface looks like it hasn't been updated in years, and the discussion forum still uses that AOL chat room font.

And I love it. I can kill hours on that site.

If I type "Fra-" into my web browser, it immediately suggests Fragrantica.

Mind you, my own name and website URL begin "Fra-" but my browser knows it's a distant second.

Fragrantica has eclipsed Francesca.

Of course I registered and made a profile on it. I'm FrancescaInFiore, "Francesca in Bloom" in Italian.

I know, it's so dorky, but it's hardly the worst. Scanning the usernames, there are a lot of puns, like "Neckromancer," and a few questionable choices like, "Smelly Finger."

I had to make a profile so I could leave my own reviews and fill out my virtual-fragrance wardrobe. That way other users can see what I have and what I like. We can make recommendations to each other. Some users even arrange perfume swaps.

But I'm not ready to meet these people in real life.

Primarily, I use it to scout out new scents at home. I can search by fragrance note, or brand, or parfumier, or any category you can imagine. When I find a perfume I'm curious about, I can read its official Fragrantica profile, see the rating it gets from users about what season they wear it in, what time of day, longevity, etc, and, finally, I pore over all the reviews of what it's like.

If it sounds good enough to try in person, I click the "for test" button and it's instantly added to my personal "for test" list in my profile page—very handy the next time I go to the fragrance department.

And so we've come full circle.

Get the coffee bean sniff-palate cleanser, because I'm going to be here for a while.

Pasta Impasse

Lisa

You know how on Facebook, people say their relationship is complicated?

Well, my relationship just got complicated.

I'm talking about my relationship with pasta.

Let me take you back in time to the dark ages, when we didn't even use the word pasta.

Back then, we called it spaghetti.

And growing up in a household of The Flying Scottolines, we had spaghetti every night for dinner.

I'm not even kidding.

I have mentioned this before but it bears repeating.

We thought spaghetti was what you had for dinner.

Sometimes we had it with meatballs, sometimes with chicken, but always spaghetti. You would think this got boring, but it never did. All my friends wanted to come to our house for dinner.

Why?

Because we had spaghetti.

On holidays we had ravioli or gnocchi, but even then, we still served it with spaghetti.

Yes, we had carbohydrates with a side of carbohydrates.

And we were as happy as clams.

Spaghetti with clams.

So naturally, I grew up loving spaghetti, and it's still the food I crave. I would eat it every night if my jeans would permit.

My sweatpants are fine with it, however.

Then, in the evolution of spaghetti history, everybody started calling it pasta, which enabled restaurants to charge three dollars more.

At about the same time, I started reading about how you should eat whole-wheat pasta because it was made of healthier ingredients.

Like it didn't have semolina.

Until then I didn't know that regular pasta was made of semolina, which sounds like a last name.

Meet Lisa Semolina, author and dog-lover.

But I read that whole-wheat spaghetti was better for you because it had more protein. I compared, and on the box, it said that regular spaghetti had seven grams of protein, but whole-wheat pasta has eight grams of protein.

You might not think that one gram makes a difference, but I never underestimate the power of one.

Not only literally.

Literally, it takes me three years to lose a single pound, so I don't take one for granted.

So I made the switch to whole-wheat spaghetti and I told myself that it tasted the same.

It didn't, but I lived with it.

I completely replaced my semolina-laden spaghetti with whole-wheat spaghetti and drowned it in tomato sauce.

Or gravy, to those of you who speak the language.

The language being South Philly.

I went happily/unhappily on my way, eating whole-wheat pasta until I saw a different type of pasta that was supposed to be even healthier, called Protein Plus.

Plus is definitely good, right?

Protein Plus pasta seems to be somewhere between whole-wheat pasta and regular pasta, and it has ten grams of protein.

Wow!

That's three more grams than seven—proof that I can subtract.

Or add.

Or get suckered in by anything.

So I bought the Protein Plus pasta, drowned that in sauce/gravy, and kept telling myself how much fun I was having.

Until I came across a new kind of pasta that was made from chickpeas, and it had thirteen grams of protein.

In other words, I hit the protein jackpot!

For a long time, I subbed that in, burying it in gravy and also mozzarella.

Obviously, we're abandoning the calorie count. I needed the mozzarella to smother the taste, which I never needed with regular pasta, which tastes awesome all by itself.

So I have more protein but also more carbs and fat.

And I have four different types of pasta in my pantry—regular, whole wheat, Protein Plus, and chickpea. On any given night, when I want pasta, I never know which one to choose.

So you see why my relationship with pasta is complicated.

But it isn't over.

Nobody divorces spaghetti.

Let's Twist Again

Lisa

They say that the definition of insanity is doing the same thing over and over and expecting a different result.

But they never met me.

I think it's the definition of adorable.

Besides, I don't do the same thing over and over—I do a different thing over and over.

Still it doesn't work out.

Because I don't work out.

I'm talking about the "Simply Fit Board—The Abs Legs Core Workout Board with a Twist."

That's the actual name of the product.

I didn't make it up.

I'm not illiterate.

I use commas.

And I'm the kind of person you would buy that actually says in the corner, As Seen On TV.

I have officially become Mother Mary.

But I don't blame her, I blame the election.

Because I had the news on most of the time during the election, and every commercial was either for a catheter, a copper waistband, or the Simply Fit Board, which is what we'll call it for short. And their commercials showed really trim women swiveling on multicolored plastic boards, i.e., getting in shape in a fun way.

And also boring a hole in the rug, but never mind.

It seemed easy, and I thought it might make some sense since I never do anything for my waist, which seems to be melting.

My core lacks core values.

I'm always on a diet but I never seem to lose weight, and yoga doesn't make me lose weight, even though now I can touch my toes.

Though I can't see them over my belly.

When I watched the commercial for the Simply Fit Board, I realized the women were doing The Twist.

Please pretend you know what The Twist is.

Google it if you're not sure. Search under, Mating Rituals of Ancient Peoples.

To save you the trouble, The Twist was a dance that people did back in the sixties, which became a dance craze.

You're going to have to look up Dance Craze, too.

Again to save the trouble, a dance is something that people did before they had smartphones to entertain them.

These were the olden days, when people made eye contact and enjoyed each other's company without taking even one selfie.

And a Dance Craze is a dance that goes viral.

The Twist was invented by a man who sang a song about it, and his name was Chubby Checker. Ironically, he was a little chubby even though he twisted all the time.

Evidently, he needed the Simply Fit Board!

So long story short, I thought the Simply Fit Board would make a nice addition to my collection of exercise equipment, which already includes an elliptical machine and a stationary bicycle, both of which remain remarkably stationary.

If not inert.

They're not only unused but ignored, even though they are in my office and I have to trip over them to get to the computer.

So the last thing I needed was more exercise equipment, but I started thinking that maybe this is one I will use.

Hope springs eternal.

So do hips.

Plus the commercial was on so many times that I started believing it, especially in comparison with the catheter commercial. If you show me something enough times on TV, I'm going to want whatever it is, *unless* it's a catheter.

So I ordered the Simply Fit Board, and when it came, it looked just like it did in the commercial. It's a curved board made of hard plastic, in my case pink, and I was so excited that I took it out of the box, jumped right on it, and slid across the rug like a drunken surfer.

Before I fell on my butt.

It turns out you need balance.

But it doesn't say on the box, Balance Not Included.

And the first thing that goes when you get older, right after your waistline, is your balance.

So I picked myself up, figured maybe I had done something wrong, and looked for the directions. Of course no product comes with directions anymore, which serves me right. I spent all of my life assembling things without using the directions, and now the world has called my bluff.

Ya happy now, Scottoline?

Then I dug deeper in the box, and at the bottom I found a DVD that said Workout DVD and User Guide on the cover. The only problem was I don't have a DVD player anymore and none of my computers have a DVD slot.

So I went to the website, but it was geared to selling you the contraption and didn't have any directions. Then I turned on the television, waited two seconds, and a commercial for Simply Fit Board came on, which was everything I had remembered.

I jumped back on the board and twisted my heart out, wobbling mightily, flailing my arms, almost tripping over, and finally falling off again.

Then I tried it barefoot and managed to stay on for two whole minutes.

But I couldn't twist that long.

Next up, the Hula Hoop!

Don't Bot with My Heart

Francesca

There is one Twitter account who has been toying with me for over a year.

The account is @WildBluePress, a publisher from Evergreen, Colorado. Nearly twelve thousand followers but following fewer than four hundred, so, discerning. I felt special when this account started following me. How had they found me? Through my writing? All the way from Colorado?

I was touched.

I followed back.

We seemed to have a lot in common. We were both in the book business. @WildBluePress favorited my animal welfare and disability rights tweets, so we agreed on the issues closest to my heart. And soon, I projected a host of wonderful traits and compatibilities onto the person behind this account, chief among them:

Friendship.

Then one day I received another notification: "@WildBluePress is now following you!"

Don't you mean, refollowing me?

This revealed it had unfollowed me, but when?

Did I say something wrong?

How long have you been feeling this way?

It was like one of those times when someone you've met many times forgets and reintroduces himself. I was the one who felt stupid.

This happens occasionally on social media, like those old, high-school friends on Facebook whom I *know* I was friends with in the past, who pop up as fresh friend requests.

Thought better of it, eh?

I accept their requests, but I note it. You weren't that nice to me in high school and you unfriended me in college, but then you see my name on a couple books and suddenly you want to be all buddy-buddy again.

I refriend, but I don't forget.

See, on social media you can get away with ghosting a conversation or relationship without word. But if you want to get away with it, you can never refriend or refollow. That's what the "mute" function is for.

But I wasn't mad at @WildBluePress, I was hurt.

Which I know is silly. Social media isn't real. Twitter is such a jumble, I'd never notice when someone unfollows me.

My own mother didn't follow me on Instagram, and neither of us realized for four years.

Twitter is particularly weird because many, if not most, of the people you follow and who follow you are strangers in real life, yet relationships can form nonetheless.

I once went out with a guy I met on Twitter. He was a writer and teacher in South Dakota. He came to New York and we went out for oysters and cocktails, then we hugged good-bye and never saw each other again.

It's a strange and wonderful world, folks.

My Twitter following is small enough that I notice my notifications when someone retweets or likes my tweet. It's a small thing, but it makes me happy. It almost makes me happier when a stranger likes it because the approval feels more earned.

The Holy Grail of Twitter is tweeting some observation that is so apt or witty or hilarious it goes *viral*.

That's like being made Prom King or Queen of Twitter.

The nadir of Twitter is going viral for saying something awful or stupid or offensive.

That's the pig's blood getting dumped on your head.

But the elusive promise of gaining a swell of popularity among strangers is why people get themselves into such trouble on Twitter.

All of these noncomics showing up at a dangerously open mic, desperate for laughs.

We think we're Chris Rock, but too many of us are Carrot Top.

Point is, these strange, fragile online connections matter to us.

So @WildBluePress bewildered me with its follows and unfollows, adding me to lists and taking me off them.

I've dated men with fewer intimacy issues.

And much like I respond with men, it made me try harder.

I assumed it was my fault. I would try to be more interesting and retweet fewer cheesy baby-animal pictures—or *more* baby-animal pictures, tell me what you want, @WildBluePress!

All the Wi-Fi access in the world, but no communication.

I never unfollowed @WildBluePress, to prove my loyalty.

I'm here for you when you're ready to let down your walls.

But when the account's behavior seemed truly random, I had a terrible thought?

Is it a bot?

I have heard of Twitterbots, robot accounts programmed with automatic posts, or set to automatically follow and engage with users that fit certain criteria. But I thought all bots and spam accounts had sexy-girl avatars and repetitive offers to "make money working from home!"

All this time, I was feeling my heart lift at my latest notification from you, but was I being played for a fool?

I feel so betrayed, I feel a country song coming on:

Your retweets meant nothing.

Your red hearts, untrue.

How could you do it, Wild Blue?

I still don't really know. I can't bring myself to ask directly. To know might hurt too much.

So, @WildBluePress, if you're reading this, I'm not like the other authors you follow.

I care.

Please follow me back.

And stay.

Built Ford Tough

Lisa

Everybody talks about how men love cars.

But so do women.

Especially this woman.

I even love trucks.

I know you're surprised. You thought I was a highly cultured member of the literati.

Oh, wait. You didn't think that?

Good.

Because what I really am is a lady who writes books for a living and lives on a farm with a bunch of crazy animals— Cavalier King Charles spaniels, cats, chickens, and horses, plus one incontinent corgi, which is a different species altogether.

By the way, if that sounds great to you, it absolutely is. It's my life's dream, made possible by the support of my beloved readers, and believe me when I tell you that I thank God for you, every day.

No kidding.

And the best thing about living on a farm is that it gives me an excuse to drive a truck. And not only that, but it's a very butch truck, which might be redundant.

It's a cherry-red Ford F-150 with a ¾-ton engine, which is powerful enough to pull a horse trailer or get me to the library.

I have to tell you, it's fun to drive around in a truck, feeling big, powerful, and generally manly. I fill its tank with gas and testosterone.

I like knowing that I can move anything I have to, and I love lending it to people when they need a truck. Because I have a truck, and I can do anything!

People always say to me, *you* have a truck?

I nod happily. You can have a truck, a brain, and ovaries— all at the same time.

They're not mutually exclusive.

Plus my truck has a snowplow on the front and a dump bed in the back, which makes it more fun to play with. It's cool to press a button to dump things out, especially if it's a load of horse manure.

Are you completely disillusioned yet?

And I never have more fun than when I'm plowing snow from my driveway in wintertime, with the radio blasting and a hot cup of coffee fogging up the windows. I will never forget the year when I got carried away and ended up plowing my whole street.

Nothing will make you feel as unstoppable as a snowplow.

I promise, you'll end up praying for snow.

Sometimes I think that driving a truck is empowerment on wheels.

Again, not even kidding.

Maybe you're secure enough and you don't need it, but I do. From time to time, I need to be reminded that I have strength and power, especially when there are setbacks. The world throws us curveballs. A friend falls ill. Somebody breaks your heart. You don't get the job you wanted.

Life can be hard and unfair, and you have to persevere.

Whenever I need bucking up, I truck up.

I take a drive around the block.

It's a way to remind my body what powerful feels like, and even though it's external, swathing me in Ford-tough military-grade steel, I can recall that feeling later, like muscle memory.

I feel the same way when I ride a horse. I'm sure there's not a woman in the world who doesn't stand a little taller after she gets out of a truck or off a horse.

And if you haven't had those experiences, I bet you feel that way after you work out or go for a run. Or after yoga.

Or after whatever you do to remind yourself that you're stronger than you think.

I'm thinking about trucks now because mine is now fifteen years old and needs to be replaced. It's dripping gunk and doing other undesirable things, and I'm going to miss it. But it gives me the chance to go truck-shopping, which for this girl, is almost as much fun as shoe-shopping.

Trucks are high heels with four-wheel drive.

So here's my advice, when the going gets rough.

Do whatever it takes to make you stand taller.

And go forward.

Women are built Ford tough.

Weeding

Lisa

You probably have heard by now that in this past election, California, Massachusetts, Nevada, and Maine legalized the recreational use of marijuana.

Are you moving?

From or to?

When I found out, I was jealous, mainly because everybody's about to become a better gardener than I am.

They grow weed, and I only grow weeds.

This is where you find out how boring a person I am, because the truth is, I never even tried marijuana.

Or, as we called it back in college, dope.

I know it's not called that anymore.

Now when something is dope, it's good.

And when something is sick, it's awesome.

Ask me anything. I'm an expert on outdated slang.

You go, girl!

Anyway, the reason I bring this up is because somebody has figured out how to grow weed that is allegedly an aphrodisiac, which is being marketed to women.

It's called Sexpot.

I'm not making that up.

I wish I were. It's almost as good a pun as Chick Wit.

Anyway, I'm always interested in products that claim to be aphrodisiacs, when we all know that the one and only aphrodisiac is a man volunteering to build you some bookshelves.

So I started to research Sexpot, which is when I learned that marijuana has different strains, strengths, and funny names, all of which was news to this weed rookie.

For example, Sexpot is apparently derived from a strain of marijuana named Mr. Nice.

Okay, now I see why it's an aphrodisiac.

Who wouldn't want to ease under the covers with Mr. Nice?

That's all we really want, isn't it, ladies?

Somebody nice.

The only guy better would be Mr. Right.

But not Mr. Right Away.

Mr. Right Away is never good in bed.

Mr. Right Away is good for picking up his socks.

Mr. Marriage Material would be ideal, but I'm not getting the impression there's any weed named after him.

Or better yet, Dr. Marriage Material.

Still, not happening.

Anyway the interesting thing I learned about Sexpot was that it has 14 percent THC, which is apparently a low amount and therefore better for women.

We always get gypped on the THC.

Evidently, the low amount of THC "allows the toker to settle into a right mellow head-space without being too high to focus on sexual sensations."

Wow.

First off, do people still say "toker"?

I remember that from the song about the midnight toker.

So maybe I'm hipper than I think.

Secondly, how is a right mellow head-space different from a mellow headspace?

And why does head-space have a hyphen?

Then I learned that Sexpot is related to cannabis lube, which is supposed to be a product that improves sex and can actually "get one's vagina high."

Really!

You know what gets my vagina high?

The King of Prussia Mall.

Chocolate cake.

Bradley Cooper.

That's about it, for now.

In truth, I can't remember the last time my vagina was high.

I suspect it's been slacking.

Well, it's definitely slack.

Then I kept researching and I found a recipe to make your own cannabis lube for your vagina, which had so many steps that it reminded me of Mother Mary's gnocchi recipe.

The main ingredient was two cups of organic extra virgin coconut oil, which I assume you could find in the organic aisle at Wegman's or in CVS, next to the Monistat.

Then you have to liquefy the coconut oil in a saucepan over low heat and add two grams of cannabis, which evidently you can buy in every state but Pennsylvania. Because the Commonwealth doesn't want a lot of high vaginas running around.

Would you?

It's a recipe for trouble.

Anyway the third step is that you have to submerge the cannabis in the coconut oil and cook it for ninety minutes, stirring occasionally.

Ninety minutes!

That's quite a commitment to vaginal lubrication.

You'd have to be either a home cook or total slut.

I mean, I don't know any woman who would bother.

We're busy!

Plus I can't think of another food that takes that amount of time and attention except for risotto, which I made once and never again. It was delicious, but so much work that I would only bother for a carbohydrate.

Not for sex.

I have priorities.

Now if I could microwave it, that would be a different story.

On the other hand, I know a better vaginal lubricant.

Bradley Cooper.

Keep Calm and Carry On

Lisa Scottoline

It's summertime, when you get to pack your bags and head off on vacation, maybe even someplace far away.

But if you're flying, you can skip the packing. Because one of the airlines just announced that they're going to limit passengers to only one carry-on bag per person, and it has to be small enough to fit under the seat.

Great idea!

I'm completely behind it.

So what if you're on vacation for a week or even two?

According to the airlines, you can wear the same thing every day.

I do that already, and I'm not even going anywhere.

In summertime, I wear a T-shirt and shorts, and in winter we're talking a fleece top and fleece pants.

I only change if I'm expecting a package. I don't want the UPS man to look at me funny.

Besides, I think the airlines are doing this to look out for us.

They don't want us to worry about our appearance.

Or our aroma.

The airlines care about us, bottom line.

Of course, they care about their bottom line as well.

I suspect they're doing this as a cost-cutting measure, but I don't understand why it costs an airline more to fly the plane if a passenger has two carry-ons rather than one. If it requires extra fuel, can it be so much extra?

I mean, back in high school, I asked my pals to chip in for gas one road trip.

But then, I graduated.

To being classy.

Doesn't an airline have to figure out how to make money by providing the services that people reasonably expect, namely that they can get on board with two bags?

Do we have to pay for the fuel, too?

How about we bring our own toilet paper?

Because this is a load of crap.

This is exactly why, when they offer me a bag of pretzels, I always take two.

Out of sheer spite.

And then I eat both bags, just to show them that it's all their fault I broke my diet.

I wonder if the airlines will announce more cost-cutting measures. If they're cutting down on the weight of clothes, why not charge extra if the passenger decides to wear pants?

Pants take up an obvious amount of extra room, and they are completely unnecessary, in my opinion.

For example, does Bradley Cooper really need to travel with pants on?

I don't think so.

How about shirts?

He doesn't need one of those either, not on my account.

I would cover him with a blanket.

Me.

But not all rules apply only to Bradley Cooper.

Some could apply to me as well.

For example, I think airlines should start charging women if they want to wear bras on board.

Take it from me, bras are completely superfluous. And given the padding and underwire in mine, I'm single-handedly weighing the plane down.

My fuel costs are 36B.

In fact, if you think big picture, there is probably a lot of dumb stuff on board a plane that we could jettison and save the airline money.

What about those flotation devices under the seat? We're never flying over water anyway, and if we are, something tells me that when we hit the water, my pancake of a seat isn't going to help my pancake of a body.

Too dark?

Okay then, how about those dumb airline magazines that nobody reads? Who really reads the Sky Mall or Hammacher Schlemmer catalogue.

(I do, because I read everything in my general vicinity, like cereal boxes. But at least I know that's weird.)

And what about that big inflatable slide that looks like so much fun?

It probably weighs a ton, but it could come in handy.

And it's an excuse to have a damn good time in an emergency.

Drunk Click

Francesca

I was working at my desk when my doorbell rang.

I opened the door to find a cardboard box sitting in my hallway, large enough to fit a person inside,

The box bore no brand logos or identifying marks, just a shipping label addressed to me.

But I wasn't expecting any package.

I tried to pick it up, but the weight of its heavy contents shifted, and I nearly dropped it. So I shuffled it into the middle of my apartment, and regarded it suspiciously.

I opened a pair of scissors, held them like a dagger, and took a breath before plunging the blade into the belly of the box.

I looked inside and recoiled with horror and despair.

Not because I didn't recognize it, but because I did.

I had purchased *cat furniture*.

In my defense, I was drunk at the time.

The memory returned to me: I had come home from being out with friends to find my cat, Mimi, clawing the arm of my couch.

Again.

"That's it!" I said, though it probably came out like, "Thazzit!"

I logged on to Amazon.com and bought the top-selling cat scratching post with one click.

Online shopping under the influence is a crime against the self.

What percentage of Jeff Bezo's fortune is attributable to drunken Amazon purchases? You know that's why they instituted "1-click" ordering.

Sober people have time for two clicks.

My buyer's remorse was twofold. First, I had completely underestimated the size of this item. I'd thought it was maybe two feet high, easy to tuck out of view.

Now I stood before a sisal-wrapped column that was nearly my height.

To be fair, I make errors of scale with online shopping when I'm clearheaded, too. Like the time I bought fishnet stockings for a Halloween costume and they arrived in a toddler size.

Why do toddler-sized fishnets exist in the first place? Never mind, I don't want to know.

The other source of regret was that, as a single woman, purchasing any large-scale cat furniture feels like an admission of defeat.

It's a monument to spinsterhood. A totem pole to protect you from a sex life.

It's the opposite of phallic symbol. It's an anti-phallic symbol.

I considered returning it, but I'd have to drag this heavy, unwieldy box to the post office. And I glanced at the once-neat lines of my chic, modern couch, now frayed to something more shabby-chic, or just shabby.

In vino veritas. I surrendered to the scratching post.

As if the indignity wasn't enough, I had to assemble it, directions not included.

If you ever want to feel like your college degree was a waste of money, try to assemble cheap furniture without directions.

After some struggling, I managed to attach the base and top in a way that was sturdy.

Mimi raised her head from where she had been sleeping on the dining table (where she is not allowed to be). To my surprise, she jumped down and sauntered over toward her present.

My heart swelled with hope. If she actually liked this thing, I take back everything I said: I'll gladly be single forever, it will be worth it.

Pleasing a man is easy; pleasing a fussy cat is satisfying.

She smelled it, bumping it with her little black nose—I held my breath.

She looked at me—I met her gaze, my eyes wide with hope.

Then she changed course, strolled right past me and over to the cardboard packaging, and flattened her body on top of it.

"No, no, look, Mimi, *this*, this is your present." I crouched beside the post and made kissy noises.

She rolled onto her back, nuzzling the cardboard with her head.

I rubbed catnip all over the post and mimicked scratching it with my own nails to show her what a delight it was.

It actually wasn't bad.

Mimi watched me do this, then began licking the cardboard.

"Okay, you win."

Since then, I've seen the sisal on the post grow more and more ragged, so I know she uses it, but only when I'm not around to see.

Because the only thing that will deny your satisfaction more than owning a giant piece of cat furniture, is owning a cat.

The Bottom Line on the Bottom-of-the-Line

Lisa

Having said how empowering it is to drive a truck, I neglected to mention how disempowering it is to bargain for one.

Is there anybody in the world who likes haggling over price?

Not me.

I hate it.

Why?

Because I usually want what I'm bargaining for.

Plus I want to be liked.

This would be the double whammy for negotiators.

Let me remind you that I was a lawyer in a former life, and I negotiated all the time. I was a badass negotiator, back then. Because I wasn't fighting for myself. I was fighting for you.

It brought out the mama bear in me.

But when I'm fighting for myself, I'm a kitten. And not one of those kittens that scratches your hand. One of those kittens that hooks its flimsy nails into your sweater and won't let go.

You have to declaw me to free yourself from my love attack.

So what happened was I went to my Ford dealership, because I liked my old bottom-of-the-line truck and I wanted to replace it with another bottom-of-the-line truck. By the way, don't think I'm being cheap. The truck is my second car, and I use it mostly to plow snow, pull horses, and tool around the block when I need self-esteem.

But the Ford dealership didn't have a bottom-of-the-line truck for me to test-drive. They offered to order one for me, but only if I promised to buy it first, without seeing or even driving it.

That struck me as a pig in a poke, truck-wise.

So I went home and started comfort-eating in front of the TV—and lo and behold, I saw a commercial for a Toyota truck, which was a bright blue like an M&M.

And I thought, why not?

I like that color and I love M&Ms.

Also, maybe I'm in a Ford rut?

I get that way with cars, food, and clothes.

The only thing I don't get that way with is husbands.

I have no problem changing things up in the Marriage Department.

But chocolate cake and I will be together forever.

To return to point, I used to think that way about Ford and I couldn't give it up easily, so I went to another Ford dealership, where they happened to have one bottom-of-the line truck, in white. I drove it around, and the Ford guys were super nice and I liked the truck okay, but I kept thinking about the blue Toyota in the commercial.

My head had been turned.

Then I did some research into Toyota trucks and I learned that they're built in the USA, which matters to me.

So on a lark, I went to a Toyota dealership, but they didn't have the bottom-of-the-line. The only truck they had was middle-of-the-line—in the M&M blue.

I test-drove it and fell in love.

And I wanted it, even though it was nicer than I needed.

Let the bargaining begin!

I never know how to start haggling, so I asked simply, "Isn't there anything better you can do on the price?"

"I have to talk to my manager," the salesman said, then went away and came back. He had taken something off the price, but it wasn't very much, and since the truck was the nicer model, it made sense that it cost more than the bottom-of-the-line Ford.

But I didn't want to give up.

I told myself to haggle like a grown-ass woman.

So I asked, "Can you sharpen your pencil?" which is something I heard someone say once. It sounds a lot better than, "Can you give it to me cheaper, please?"

The salesman went away again and when he came back, his pencil was sharper, but not sharp enough. The truck was still too expensive.

I came to my senses, and my inner monologue kicked in:

I didn't need the nicer truck. It was right that the nicer truck cost more than I wanted to pay. You can't get middle-of-the-line for a bottom-of-the-line price, especially not if you're a lousy negotiator like me.

"Thank you, but no." I picked up my purse, rose to go, and started walking toward the door.

At which point all hell broke loose.

The salesman started running toward me, and so did another guy in a tie, and both men called my name, so I turned around.

"I'm the manager," said the guy in the tie. "Please, come back and sit down. Let me give you our blowout price."

BLOWOUT PRICE?!

"Okay," I said calmly, knowing that it probably would not be anywhere near what I was willing to pay.

So we sat down.

And very dramatically, the manager took out a piece of paper and actually wrote BLOWOUT PRICE in a Sharpie, and next to that, he wrote a blowout price. It wasn't as low as I wanted, but it wasn't as high as before.

It was the Goldilocks of truck prices.

By the way, did I mention that the truck was M&M blue?

And made in the USA?

Dear Reader, I bought my dream truck!

My new blue truck sits in my driveway, right underneath my red American flag.

Red, white, and blowout price.

I realized later that I didn't have to say anything to get the better deal.

I just had to leave.

So what is the moral of the story—or even of this book?

Sometimes you do the right thing, even when you have no idea what you're doing.

Even though your brain is saying: YOU CAN'T NEGOTIATE. YOU CAN'T EVEN SWIM. YOU NEED A LIFEGUARD.

We really are our own lifeguard, in the end.
Our feet will walk us right out the door.
Or wherever we want to go.
May you get the truck of your dreams.
May you get whatever you wish for.
You deserve nothing less.
Because you are top-of-the-line.

Acknowledgments

Lisa and Francesca

Time for thank-yous! We love and thank St. Martin's Press for supporting this entire series from day one to bestsellerdom. The biggest thanks go to Coach Jen Enderlin, our terrific editor, and major thanks to the brilliant John Sargent, Don Weisberg, Sally Richardson, Jeff Dodes, Jeff Capshew, Lisa Senz, Brant Janeway, Erica Martirano, George Witt, John Edwards, Jeanette Zwart, Dori Weintraub, Tracey Guest, John Karle, Stephanie Davis, Brian Heller, Michael Storrings, Anne-Marie Tallberg, Sara Goodman, Kerry Nordling, Elizabeth Wildman, Caitlin Dareff, Talia Sherer, Kim Ludlum, and all the wonderful sales reps. We appreciate you all!

We'd also like to thank St. Martin's audiobook division for letting us record our own audiobook of this volume, which we love doing. Thanks to the terrific Mary Beth Roche, our director Laura Wilson, and Samantha Edelson. We love audiobooks!

Huge thanks and love to Lisa's amazing agent, Robert Gottlieb of the Trident Media Group, and his awesome digital team: Nicole Robson, Emily Ross, Caitlin O'Beirne, and Alicia Granstein. Equally huge thanks and love to Francesca's terrific agents, Andrea Cirillo, Amy Tannenbaum, and Rebecca Scherer of the Jane Rotrosen Agency—you are guiding lights. Thanks to *The Philadelphia Inquirer*, which carries our "Chick Wit" column, and to our new editor Reid Tuvim.

One of the best people in the whole entire world is our bestie/honorary aunt/resident therapist/genius assistant Laura Leonard. Laura, thank you so much for all of your great comments and suggestions to these stories. We owe you and love you, forever.

Love to our girlfriends! Lisa would like to thank Nan Daley, Paula Menghetti, Sandy Steingard, and Franca Palumbo. Francesca would like to thank Rebecca Harrington, Katy Andersen, Courtney Yip, Lauren Donahoe, Janie Stolar, and right-hand man, Ryder Kessler. We're blessed in all of you.

Family is the heart of this book, because family is the heart of everything. Special thanks and love to Brother Frank. We still miss Mother Mary and Father Frank Scottoline, though they are with us always.

Finally, a massive thank-you to our readers. You have taken this series to your heart, and so touched ours. Nothing makes us happier.

We are truly honored.

Read on for an excerpt from Lisa Scottoline's
next novel

EXPOSED

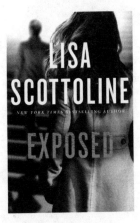

Chapter One

Mary DiNunzio stepped off the elevator, worried. Her father and his friends looked over from the reception area, their lined faces stricken. They'd called her to say they needed a lawyer but until now, she hadn't been overly concerned. Their last lawsuit was against the Frank Sinatra Social Society of South Philly on behalf of the Dean Martin Fan Club of South Philly. Luckily Mary had been able to settle the matter without involving Tony Bennett.

"Hi, Pop." Mary crossed the lobby, which was otherwise empty. Marshall, their receptionist, wasn't at her desk, though she must've already gotten in. The aroma of fresh coffee filled the air, since Marshall knew that Mary's father and his fellow octogenarians ran on caffeine and Coumadin.

"HIYA, HONEY!" her father shouted, despite his hearing aids. Everyone was used to Mariano "Matty" DiNunzio talking loudly, which came off as enthusiastic rather than angry. On the table next to him sat a white box of pastries, as the DiNunzios didn't go anywhere empty-handed, even to a law firm. The box hadn't been opened, so whatever was bothering him was something even saturated fats couldn't cure.

"Hey, Mare!" "Hi, Mary!" "*Buongiorno, Maria!*" said his friends The Three Tonys, like a Greek—or more accurately Roman—chorus. They got up to greet her, rising slowly on replacement knees, like hammers on a piano with sticky keys. Her father had grown up with The Tonys; Tony "From-Down-The-Block"

LoMonaco, "Pigeon" Tony Lucia, and Tony "Two Feet" Pensiera, which got shortened to "Feet," so even his nickname had a nickname. It went without saying that naming traditions in South Philly were *sui generis,* which was Latin for completely insane. The Tonys went everywhere with her father and sometimes helped her on her cases, which was like having a secret weapon or a traveling nightmare.

"Good morning, Pop." Mary reached her father and gave him a big hug. He smelled the way he always did, of hard soap from a morning shave and the mothballs that clung to his clothes. He and The Tonys were dressed in basically the same outfit—a white short-sleeved shirt, baggy Bermuda shorts, and black-socks-with-sandals—like a barbershop quartet gone horribly wrong.

"THANKS FOR SEEIN' US, HONEY." Her father hugged her back, and Mary loved the solidity of his chubby belly. She would move mountains for him, but it still wouldn't be enough to thank him for being such a wonderful father. Both of her parents loved her to the marrow, though her mother could be as protective as a mother bear, if not a mother Tyrannosaurus rex.

"No problem." Mary released him, but he looked away, which was unlike him. "You okay, Pop?"

"SURE, SURE." Her father waved her off with an arthritic hand, but Mary was concerned. His eyes were a milky brown behind his bifocals, but troubled.

"What is it?"

"YOU'LL SEE. YOUR MOTHER SAYS HI."

Just then Feet raised his slack arms, pulled Mary close to his chest, and hugged her so hard that he jostled his Mr. Potatohead glasses. He, too, seemed agitated, if affectionate. "Mare, thank you for making the time for us."

"Of course, I'm happy to see you."

"I appreciate it. You're such a good kid." Feet righted his thick trifocals, repaired with Scotch tape at one corner. His round eyes were hooded, his nose was bulbous, and he was completely bald, with worry lines that began at his eyebrows and looked more worried than usual.

"Mary!" Tony-From-Down-The-Block reached for her with typical vigor, the youngest of the group, at eighty-three. He worked out, doing a chair-exercise class at the senior center, and was dating again, as evidenced by his hair's suspicious shade of reddish-brown, like oxblood shoe polish. He gave her a hug, and Mary breathed in his Paco Rabanne and BenGay, a surprisingly fragrant combination.

"Good to see you." Mary let him go and moved on to hug Pigeon Tony, an Italian immigrant with a stringy neck, who not only raised homing pigeons but looked like one. Pigeon Tony was barely five feet tall and bird-thin, with a smooth bald head and round brown-black eyes divided by a nose shaped like a beak. In other words, adorable.

"*Come stai, Maria?*" Pigeon Tony released her with a sad smile, and Mary tried to remember her Italian.

"*Va bene, grazie. E tu?*"

"*Cosi, cosi,*" Pigeon Tony answered, though he'd never before said anything but *bene*. You didn't have to speak Italian to know there was a problem, and Mary turned to address the foursome.

"So what's going on, guys? How can I help you?"

"IT'S NOT ABOUT US," her father answered gravely.

Feet nodded, downcast. "It's about Simon."

"Oh no, what's up?" Mary loved Feet's son Simon, who was her unofficial cousin, since The Tonys were her unofficial uncles.

"He's not so good."

"What's the matter? Is it Rachel?" Mary felt a pang of fear. Simon's wife Ellen died four years ago of an aneurysm, and Simon had become a single father of an infant, Rachel. When Rachel turned three, she was diagnosed with leukemia but was in remission.

"Simon will explain it. Oh, here he comes now!" Feet turned to the elevator just as the doors opened and Simon stepped out, looking around to orient himself.

"Hey, honey!" Mary called to him, hiding her dismay. He looked tired, with premature gray threaded through his dark curly hair, and though he had his father's stocky build, he'd lost weight. His navy sport jacket hung on him and his jeans were too big. She hadn't seen him in a while, since he was busy with Rachel, though they'd kept in touch by email.

"Hi, Mary!" Simon strode toward her, and Mary reached him with a hug, since she could only imagine what he'd been going through, not only with the baby, but losing Ellen. Mary herself had been widowed young, after the murder of her first husband Mike. Even though she was happily remarried, Mike was a part of her and always would be, which suited her and her new husband Anthony just fine.

"It's so good to see you, honey." Mary released him, and Simon brightened.

"This office is so nice, with your name on the sign."

"Believe me, I'm as surprised as you are." Mary could see Simon was happy for her and felt a new rush of affection for him. "How's the baby?"

"I'll fill you in later." Simon's smile stiffened. "I just moved her to CHOP."

Mary wondered why Rachel had been moved, but it wasn't the time to ask. CHOP was the Children's Hospital of Philadelphia, one of the best in the country. Mary's heart went out to him. "I'm praying for her, and so is my mother. She's got the novenas on overdrive."

"I know, and she sends me Mass cards, God bless her." Simon's smile returned. "I tell our rabbi, I'll take all the help I can get."

"Exactly. She prayed for me to make partner."

"Ha! Anyway, thanks for seeing me on such short notice. Are you sure you have the time?"

"Totally. My first appointment isn't until ten thirty." Mary motioned him out of the reception area. "Let's go to the conference room."

"Okay." Simon fell into step beside her, followed by her father, The Tonys, and the pastry box, which gave Mary pause. Simon was a potential client, and she wouldn't ordinarily have a client consultation with an audience, blood-related or not.

"Simon, did you want to talk alone?" she asked him, stopping in the hallway. "What we say is confidential, and it's your call whether your dad or anybody else comes in with us. They can wait in—"

Feet interrupted, "No, I wanna be there, Mare. I know what he's gonna tell you, we all do."

Tony-From-Down-The-Block snorted. "Of course we'll be there. Feet's his father, and I taught him how to ride a bike."

"I CHANGED HIS DIAPERS!"

Mary looked over, skeptically. "When, Pop?"

"THAT ONE TIME, I FORGET." Her father held up the pastry box by its cotton string. "PLUS I GOT BREAKFAST."

Pigeon Tony kept his own counsel, his dark gaze darting from Simon to Mary, and she suspected that he understood more than he let on, regardless of the language.

Simon smiled crookedly. "Mary, you didn't think we were going to shake them, did you? It's okay. They can come with."

"THIS WAY, I KNOW WHERE IT IS!" Her father lumbered off, down the hallway.

"Of course, we're all going!" Feet said, at his heels. "We're family. We're all family!"

"*Andiamo!*" said Pigeon Tony.

Mary led them down the hallway and into the conference room, where Thomas Eakins's rowing prints lined the warm white walls and fresh coffee had been set up on the credenza. The far side of the room was glass, showing an impressive view of the Philadelphia skyline thick with humidity. July was a bad-hair month in Philly, and Mary was already damp under her linen dress.

She closed the conference-room door, glancing at Simon, who perched unhappily on the edge of his chair. He'd always been one of the smartest and nicest kids in the neighborhood, affable enough to make friends even though he was one of the few that didn't go to parochial school. He'd gone to Central High, and the Pensieras were Italian Jews, but the religious distinction made no difference as far as the neighborhood was concerned. The common denominator was homemade tomato sauce.

"Simon, would you like coffee?" Mary set down her purse and messenger bag while her father and The Tonys surged to the credenza.

"No, thanks. Let's get started." Simon sat down catty-corner to the head of the table.

"Agree." Mary took the seat, slid her laptop from her bag, and powered it up while her father and The Tonys yakked away, pouring coffee and digging into the pastry box.

"MARE, YOU TWO START WITHOUT US. DON'T WAIT ON US."

Mary pulled her laptop from her bag, fired it up, and opened a file, turning to Simon. "So, tell me what's going on."

"Okay." Simon paused, collecting his thoughts. "Well, you remember, I'm in sales at OpenSpace, and we make office cubicles. We have different designs and price points, though we also customize. We did $9 million in sales last fiscal year and we have forty-five employees, including manufacturing and administrative, in Horsham."

"How long have you worked for them, again?"

"Twelve years, almost since I graduated Temple, and—" Simon flushed, licking lips that had gone suddenly dry. "Well, I just got fired."

"Oh, no," Mary said, surprised. Simon was smart and hardworking, a success from the get-go. "When did this happen?"

"Two days ago, Tuesday. July 11."

"Why?" Mary caught Feet's stricken expression, and her father and the others had gone quiet.

"They said it was my performance. But I don't think that's the real reason."

"What do you think?" Mary's mind was already flipping through the possible illegal reasons, which weren't many. Pennsylvania was a right-to-work state, which meant that an employee could be fired at will, for any or no reason, as long as it wasn't discriminatory.

"Honestly, my performance is great. I'm one of the top reps. I've gotten great reviews and bonuses for years. Things started to go south after Rachel was diagnosed. The final straw for them was—" Simon hesitated, and Feet came over and placed a hand on his shoulder.

"Son, the baby's going to be fine. We're all praying, and she's got good doctors. *Great* doctors."

"Thanks, Dad." Simon returned his attention to Mary, her gaze newly agonized. "I didn't let people know, but awhile ago, Rachel relapsed again and she has to have a bone marrow transplant. That's why she got moved to CHOP."

"Oh no, I'm sorry to hear that." Mary felt her chest tighten with emotion, but she didn't want to open any floodgates, especially with Feet, her father, and the others. Now she understood why they'd been so upset. Simon was in dire straits, with Rachel so ill and now him out of a job.

"Obviously, I wish the chemo had worked, but I feel great about the BMT Team at CHOP. They specialize in ALL." Simon caught himself. "Sorry about the lingo. BMT stands for Blood and Marrow Transplant Team and ALL is acute lymphoblastic leukemia, which is what she has."

"I can't imagine how hard this is to go through, for all of you."

"We're doing the best we can. My dad's there all the time, so it helps when I have to work." Simon managed a shaky smile. "It's just that as a father, you feel so helpless. I'm mean, it sounds cliché, but it's true. I know, I *live* it. You have hope, but no control. None at all. Well, you get it. You know, you see. She has to be okay."

"She will be," Feet said quietly, and Mary's father, Pigeon Tony, and Tony-From-Down-The-Block walked over, their lined faces masks of sorrow and fear. They stood motionless behind him, having forgotten about the coffee and pastries.

"SIMON, WE'LL HELP ANY WAY WE CAN. WON'T WE, MARE?"

"Yes, we will," Mary answered, meaning it. She patted Simon's hand again.

Tony-From-Down-The-Block chimed in, "We're going to get through this together." He gestured at Pigeon Tony. "He's gonna make some baked ziti for you, Simon. He's an excellent cook, like, gourmet. All you gotta do is put it in the microwave."

"Thanks, guys." Simon turned around, then faced Mary. "Anyway, I think that's the reason why they fired me."

Mary blinked. "How so?"

"Well, when Rachel was first diagnosed, my boss Todd was really nice about it. I have decent benefits and they covered Rachel. I took out a second mortgage to cover what it doesn't. The meds are astronomical." Simon leaned over, urgent. "But OpenSpace is self-insured up to $250,000, which means that their insurance policy doesn't reimburse them until their employee medical expenses reach that amount. They have to pay out of pocket until then."

"Understood. It's like a deductible." Mary knew the basics of employment benefits.

"Exactly." Simon nodded. "But Rachel's bills alone are so high that the insurance company is going to raise the premiums."

"I see, and are the premiums going up?"

"I don't know, but I'm getting ahead of myself. After Rachel's first round of chemo, my boss Todd kept asking me how Rachel was. I thought he was interested, like, being nice. He has a ten-year-old daughter. But then he made comments about the bills when I submitted them. And then when the first bills for chemo came in, for seven grand, he reduced my territory from three states—Jersey, Pennsylvania, and Delaware—to just Delaware."

Mary didn't understand something. "What does it matter that your territory was reduced?"

"A reduction in my territory means I can't make my sales quotas. Not only that, but the territory he gave me was more residential and had less businesses, so there was no way I could ever make quota." Simon flushed. "I tried, but no matter what I did, I was only selling a fraction of the units. For the first time in twelve years, I didn't make quota."

Mary put it together. "So your sales go down and your performance suffers."

"Right." Simon nodded. "Todd was trying to force me out, hoping that I would quit, but I didn't. I love my accounts, my reps, and my job, and I need the job."

"Of course."

"So when Rachel's pediatric oncologist told me she needed the transplant and referred me to CHOP, I told Todd and he asked how much it was going to cost. At the time, I didn't know the costs of the transplant, but the donor search alone cost like $60,000 to $100,000, and I told him that."

"To search for a match? Why does that cost so much? It didn't cost that much when we tried before, did it?" Mary was referring to a previous time, when Rachel had been considered for a bone marrow transplant and they had all registered as donors, by giving cheek swabs to collect DNA. None of them had been matches.

"It's not the costs of donating, it's the costs of finding a donor. The hospital has to contact the Bone Marrow Donor Registry to get a list of potential matches, but they have to test at least six potential donors to get one that's a perfect match. Each test costs six to nine grand. It adds up fast."

"Oh, man." Mary hadn't realized.

"Luckily, CHOP found us a match, changed Rachel's chemo protocol, and got her into remission. You have to be in remission to do the transplant."

"That's sounds like a Catch-22."

"I know, but it isn't. I'll fill you in another time. Anyway, when I told Todd that Rachel needed the transplant, he fired me the next week, supposedly because I didn't make quota—for one month. The first time in twelve years."

"So it was a pretext because they didn't want to pay for Rachel's expenses? And they didn't want their premiums to go up?"

"I think so."

"That's heartless." Mary felt a surge of anger, the kind she always felt when somebody had been wronged. But here, it had happened to someone she knew and loved. Simon. And Rachel.

Feet shook his head. "They're bastards!"

"WHAT KIND A PEOPLE FIRE YOU BECAUSE YOU GOT A SICK KID? THEY SHOULD BURN IN HELL!"

"*Disgrazia!*"

Simon shook his head. "The irony is that OpenSpace wouldn't have had to pay another penny. CHOP worked with me and Aetna, and since I'm a Pennsylvania resident and the illness is life-threatening, I can use secondary insurance like the CAT fund and Medicaid. They cover the costs of the transplant, which is astronomical."

"How much does a bone marrow transplant cost?"

"A million bucks."

"Whoa, are you kidding?" Mary said, shocked.

"No, start to finish, it's almost a year-long process, and you can't imagine the expertise and care it takes."

"I bet." Mary got back on track. "Do you remember the comment your boss Todd made to you, about how much it was costing?"

"Yes, and I even have proof. I wrote down every time Todd said something to me about her bills. I didn't want to write it on my phone because it's company-issued." Simon reached into his sport jacket, pulled out a moleskin notebook, and set it down. "I can show you right here, when and where."

"Great." Mary picked up the notebook, opened it, and glanced at Simon's characteristically neat writing, with dates and times noted. "Simon, what's your boss's full name?"

"Todd Eddington."

Mary made a note. "How long has he been your boss and what's his job title?"

"He's sales manager. I've reported to him for twelve years." Simon swallowed hard. "I thought we were friends. I know his ex-wife, Cheryl. They were both good to Ellen." Simon's voice trailed off, but Mary wanted to keep him on the case.

"So did Todd make the decision or did somebody else?"

"He does. He makes a recommendation upstairs, to hire or fire, and it gets rubber-stamped by the president, Mike Bashir."

Mary made a note of the name.

"So is it legal, what they did?" Simon leaned over. "It seems so wrong to me. I understand that a transplant costs a lot, but they're going gangbusters and I worked for them for twelve years. Can they get away with this?"

"Not in my book. We can sue them for this, and we should, right away." Mary knew disability law as a result of her growing special-education practice and she was already drafting a complaint in her mind. She loved it when the law actually did justice, which happened less frequently than God intended.

"So it's illegal?" Simon leaned forward, newly urgent.

"Yes. There's a federal law, the Americans with Disabilities Act, and it prevents discrimination in employment based on disability or illness. So for example, you can't fire somebody because they have cancer—"

"But how does that apply to me? I'm not the one with cancer, Rachel is."

"I know, but the law has a special provision that applies here, though it's not well-known. In fact, there's very little case law on it, but it applies to us." Mary started searching online for the statute. "It's called the 'association provision' and it forbids employment discrimination on the basis of an illness contracted by people who are *associated* with the insured employee, like their family."

"Really?" Simon's eyes widened with hope.

"Yes, under the ADA, an employer is prohibited from—" Mary found the statute and started reading aloud—" 'excluding or otherwise denying equal jobs or benefits to a qualified individual because of the known disability of an individual with whom the qualified individual is known to have a relationship or association.' "

"MARE, WE DON'T GET THE LEGALESE!"

Mary explained, "It means Simon is a qualified individual under the law and he is associated with Rachel. In other words, Simon's company can't fire him because she got sick and her medical expenses are going to cost them. I have to research the cases and get more facts from you, but I think we have an excellent case here."

"That's great!" Simon threw his hands in the air.

"Thank God!" Feet cheered, and Tony-From-Down-The-Block, Pigeon Tony, and Mary's father burst into chatter, all at once. "*Bravissima, Maria!*" "Way to go, Mare! Go get 'em!"

"MARE, I KNEW YOU'D KNOW WHAT TO DO! I'M SO PROUD A YOU!" Her father shuffled over and kissed the top of her head. "THANK GOD YOU'RE SO SMART! AND BEAUTIFUL!"

"Aw, Pop." Mary flushed, relieved. She couldn't have lived with herself if she couldn't help Simon and Rachel, fighting for her life. If there was any reason she had become a lawyer, this was it. To help families, children, and the community as a whole. She felt as if she had finally found her niche in special-education and disability law and lately she'd come to work happier than ever before.

Simon beamed. "Mary, that's so amazing. How does that work? Do you think I could get my job back? I really need to work."

"Okay, hold on." Mary put up her hand. "I have to study your notebook and do my research before I can answer any of these questions for sure. And the procedure under the law is that before we go to court, we have to file a complaint with the EEOC, the Equal Employment Opportunity Commission first. Then they give us a right-to-sue letter and we can go to court. As far as remedy, I don't know if you can get your job back, but why would you want it? Do you have an employment contract or a non-compete?"

"Yes, for two years, and it covers the mid-Atlantic states. So now I can't work in sales in the area but I can't move out of the area because of Rachel being at CHOP."

Mary saw his dilemma. "Okay, we'll see what we can do. We might be able to get a decent settlement, then you can stay home with Rachel during her treatment."

"But what about her medical expenses?"

"You buy COBRA with the settlement money. That covers you both for eighteen months and you'll find another job when you free up more."

"That would be best of all! I don't know how to thank you, Mary." Simon broke into a huge smile.

Her father grinned. "HOW MUCH CAN YOU GET HIM, MARE?"

Feet chimed in, "Yeah, how much?"

Mary waved them off. "Don't get ahead of yourselves. I need to know more before we make a settlement demand and I want to see the notebook, so I understand exactly what happened."

Simon nodded, excited. "So you'll take my case, Mary? Do you have the time?"

"Of course." Mary mentally cleared her calendar. She didn't have anything as pressing as this. This was for family.

"Thank you so much!" Simon squeezed her hand. "And I just want to say up front that I'm paying you for this. I'm not expecting you to represent me for free."

"YOUR MONEY'S NO GOOD HERE. YOU KNOW THAT."

"Simon, my father's right," Mary said, meaning it. She'd have to tell her partner Bennie Rosato, but the days were over when she'd have to ask for permission.

"What do we do next?" Simon checked his watch. "I should get over to the hospital."

Feet nodded. "Simon sleeps there, and we trade off. We like to be there when she's up."

Tony-From-Down-The-Block added, "So she knows she's not alone."

"OF COURSE SHE'S NOT ALONE!" Mary's father said, and she saw his eyes begin to glisten, so she rose.

"Okay, then. Let me get started so we can get a demand letter out right away. See if we can get this settled without having to file suit."

"Think we can?" Simon stood up, his entire demeanor improved. He held his head higher and squared his shoulders.

"I can't guarantee it, but I feel good." Mary gave him a reassuring hug and gathered him, Feet, her father, the remaining Tonys, and the untouched pastry while they all exchanged "goodbyes, "thank-yous," and "love-yous." Then she ushered them out of the conference room, down the hall, and into the elevator, giving her father one final hug.

"Mary, thanks so much!" Simon called to her.

"BYE, HONEY! LOVE YOU!"

"Love you, too!" Mary glimpsed her father's eyes begin to glisten as the elevator doors slid closed. Something was still bothering him, but she didn't know what or why. The doors had sealed shut and the elevator rattled downward, leaving her to her own thoughts. She felt so good that she could help him and Rachel, but so awful that the baby needed the transplant. Only four years old, and her young life had been a series of tests and chemo, needle pricks and IV ports. It couldn't be possible that children suffered so much, yet she knew it happened every day, in every hospital in the country.

The other elevator doors slid open, and inside was Bennie Rosato, whose appearance never failed to intimidate Mary. Maybe it was because Bennie was her former boss and a superlawyer with a national reputation, or the fact that Bennie was six feet tall and towered over Mary, or the fact that Bennie always wore a khaki power suit, or that her curly blonde hair was always in an unruly topknot, proof that she was far too sensible to care about anything as dumb as hair.

"Good morning," Mary said, as Bennie flashed a confident smile, which was the only kind she had.

"Hey, DiNunzio. I mean, Mary. What are you doing, standing here?"

"I just met with a new client," Mary answered, faking a smile.

"Tough case? You look upset." Bennie strode toward the reception desk, and Mary fell in step beside her, telling herself not to be nervous around her own partner, for no reason. Or maybe for four reasons, as above.

"Yes, tough case." Mary was thinking of Rachel.

"Tough on the law?"

"No it's just sad. On the law, it's a winner. A sales rep got fired because his daughter needs a bone marrow transplant." Mary summarized it like a legal headnote since Bennie was in a hurry.

"Ouch." Bennie grimaced as she walked. "Go get 'em, tiger."

"It's totally illegal under the association provision of the ADA. I'm hoping for a quick settlement."

"Who's the defendant?"

"Some cubicle manufacturer."

"Not OpenSpace." Bennie stopped, frowning under the gleaming Rosato & DiNunzio plaque.

"Yes, why? How did you know?"

"OpenSpace is the biggest cubicle manufacturer in the area, and you can't sue them. I represent their parent company."

"I don't understand." Mary's mouth went dry.

"You're conflicted out of the case, and I didn't hear what I just heard. Decline the representation."